the fortune telling kit

chris morgan

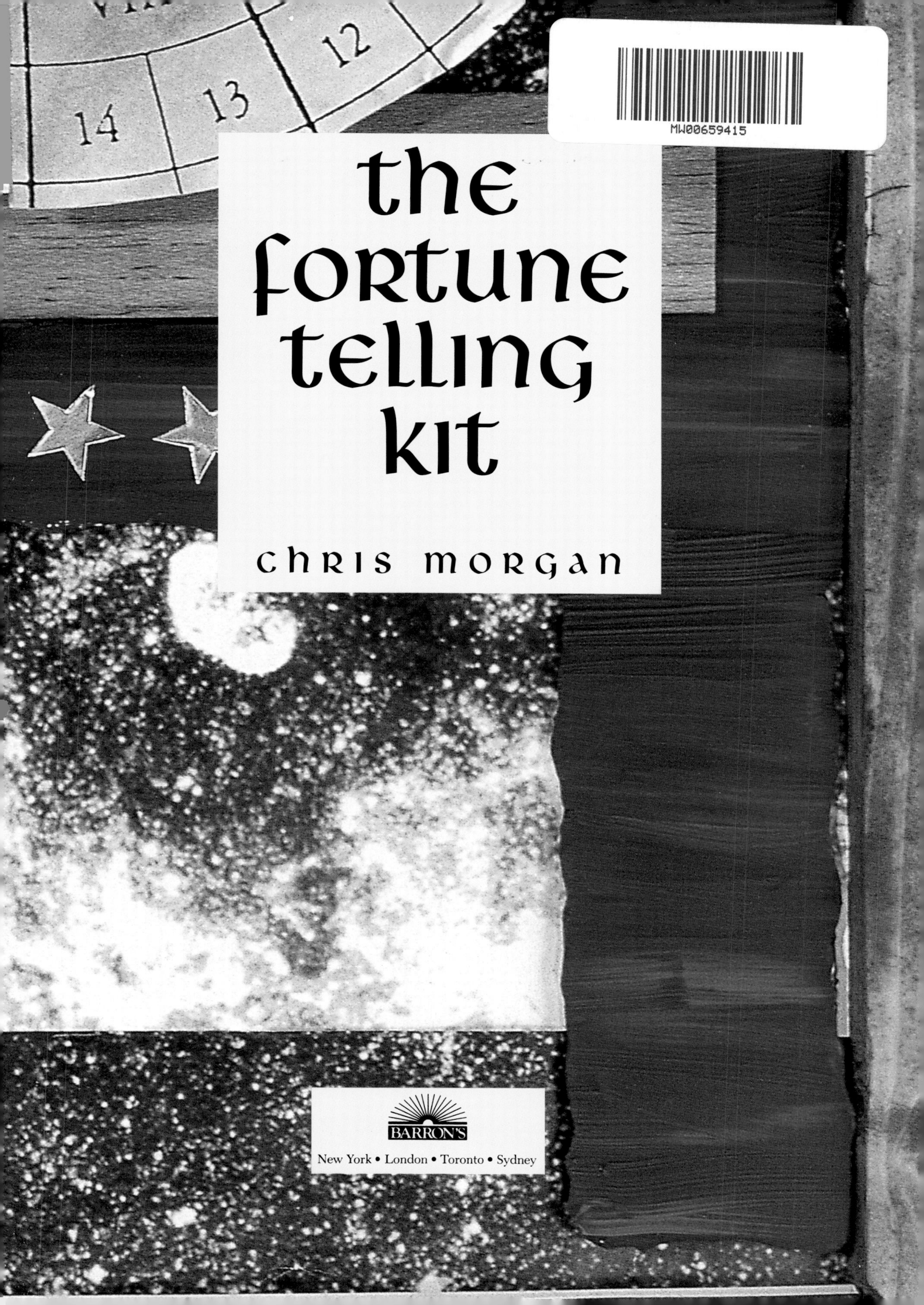

BARRON'S
New York • London • Toronto • Sydney

A Quarto Book

First U.S. edition published in 1996 by
Barron's Educational Series, Inc.

All inquiries should be addressed to:
Barron's Educational Series, Inc.
250 Wireless Boulevard,
Hauppauge, NY 11788

Library of Congress Catalog Card No.:
96-842
International Standard Book No.:
0-8120-9757-2 (book)
0-8120-8469-1 (package)

Library of Congress Cataloging-in-Publication Data
Morgan, Chris John Kear.
Fortune Telling Kit / Chris John Kear Morgan
– 1st US ed.
p. cm.
"A Quarto Book"
ISBN 0-8120-9757 (book)
ISBN 0-8120-8469-1 (package)
1. Fortune-telling 2. Divination I. Title
BF1861.M67 1996
133.3–dc20 96-842
CIP

DESIGNED AND PRODUCED BY
Quarto Publishing plc
The Old Brewery
6 Blundell Street
London N7 9BH, UK

SENIOR EDITOR Michelle Pickering
COPY EDITOR Ralph Hancock
SENIOR ART EDITOR Clare Baggaley
LAYOUT Annie Moss
MAC ARTIST John Fowler
CHAPTER OPENERS Jan Ostrowski
ETCHINGS Juliet Dallas-Conte
ILLUSTRATIONS Neil Ballpit
PHOTOGRAPHERS Paul Forrester,
Laura Wickenden
PICTURE RESEARCHER Susannah Jayes
PICTURE RESEARCH MANAGER
Giulia Hetherington
ART DIRECTOR Moira Clinch
EDITORIAL DIRECTOR Mark Dartford

Typeset by Type Technique,
121A Cleveland Street, London
Manufactured in Hong Kong by Regent
Publishing Services Ltd
Printed in Hong Kong by Winner Offset
Printing Factory Limited

contents

introduction

Many people – including you, it seems – are extremely interested in what the future has in store for them. They want to know how much money they can expect to have, how healthy they will be, what job they will have, whether they will be lucky enough to find a suitably loving partner, and whether they will have children. Indeed, some people are so desperate to obtain this information that they pay for sessions with fortune tellers of many kinds. Often they attend regularly, to see if their future has altered or to obtain guidance on overcoming a problem.

This kit helps you to practice these fortune-telling techniques for yourself, at home. It describes all the methods of divination that are popular in the western hemisphere today, all of which are traditional, and some are very ancient.

The 1980s and 1990s have been a time of great change in fortune telling. Not only has there been a great resurgence of interest in the subject, but all the traditional methods have been touched by technological advances. Instead of visiting practitioners for readings by tarot, crystal ball, runestones, or playing cards, you can now get instant answers over the telephone. Or you can buy inexpensive software for your home computer that will prepare accurate astrological birth charts, or forecasts based on numerology or the I Ching.

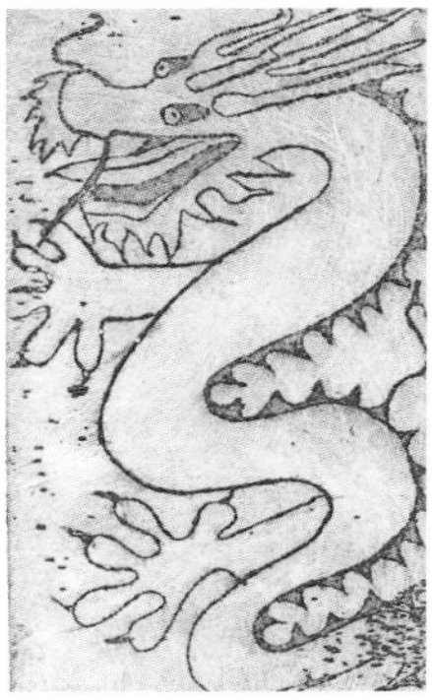

Is it possible for mere software to have the sensitivity of human intuition? Can you feel the same about a reading given over the telephone as you might about one given in the atmospheric surroundings of a psychic's studio? It is all a matter of confidence; some people prefer the new methods, some the old.

New methods are, in fact, proliferating – and one certain prediction is that the trend will continue. Name any traditional system of fortune telling, and you will find that there is a new variation, just a little different – but copyrighted. It may claim association with a traditional method because the name sounds convincing, yet it will also claim to be new, because that sells. There are decks of cards based on the I Ching; so-called oracles based on tantric philosophy or on the roll of dice; "magic" stones that are not quite the same as runestones. And there are all manner of cards for divination that are neither tarot packs nor ordinary playing cards but akin to one or both. In general, all these methods are simple and come complete with exact instructions: They leave very little room for imagination or intuition.

We have not made that mistake in this book. For each major form of divination, we offer a broad overview followed by instructions on the basic techniques and, where appropriate, a list of the meanings of various signs. This gives you a sound basis to begin your study of the method, from which you can progress as you choose. In any kind of divination that is worth taking seriously, there is no substitute for the power of the human mind – your mind.

kit components

The fortune telling kit comes complete with tarot cards, I Ching coins, and runestones, together with this book, containing full instructions for their use and for many other divination methods.

This drawstring bag is used to hold the runestones while making a reading and also for their safe storage.

Three Chinese I Ching coins are necessary to generate the six-line hexagrams whose meanings appear on pages 16–17.

The 25 runestones are etched with the runic alphabet, interpretations of which are listed on page 21.

The twenty-two Major Arcana tarot cards can be spread in a variety of ways, as detailed on page 13.

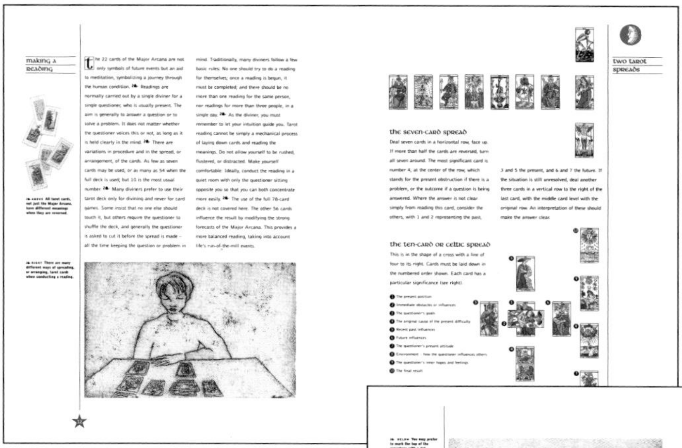

Charts, diagrams, and illustrations give detailed information about each fortune-telling method.

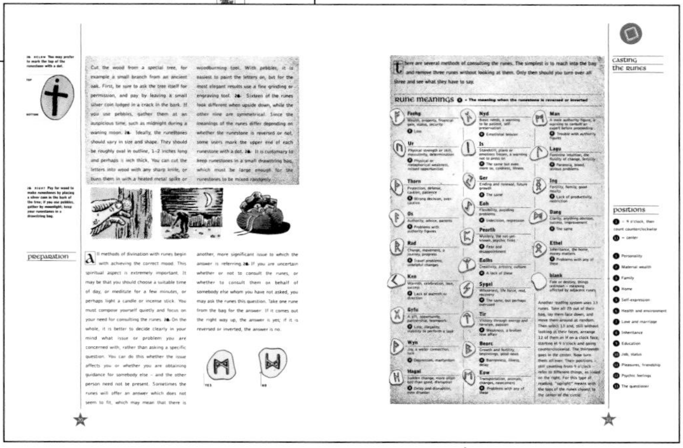

Concise interpretations for each divination method are listed for easy reference when conducting a reading.

The Fortune Telling Kit is the ideal introduction to the vast array of divination methods that are practiced today. With easy-to-follow instructions and clear, concise interpretations, it is both informative and enjoyable to use. The Kit contains a full set of runestones together with a drawstring bag, 22 Major Arcana tarot cards in a traditional design, and 3 authentic Chinese I Ching coins. Together with the Kit book, you will be able to explore these and many other divination methods. Beautifully designed and illustrated, **The Fortune Telling Kit** is the ideal companion for those who wish to discover what the future holds in store.

the tarot

THE TAROT IS A SPECIAL DECK OF PLAYING CARDS, WITH DIFFERENT SUITS FROM THOSE OF STANDARD PACKS, AND AUGMENTED BY THE ADDITION OF 22 POWER CARDS, KNOWN AS THE MAJOR ARCANA. IT IS POSSIBLE TO PLAY SPECIALLY DESIGNED GAMES WITH THEM, BUT THEIR MAIN USE IS FOR DIVINATION.

The origins of the tarot are obscure, but it was probably brought into western Europe during the early Middle Ages – perhaps by crusaders returning from the Holy Land, or by wandering bands of gypsies.

The older and more traditional packs depict life at that time. It seems that the Major Arcana cards have always been pictorial, and early hand-painted decks were attractive miniature works of art. ❧ Perhaps it is this pictorial aspect, as much as the mystique of divination, which has made the tarot increasingly popular during the last few decades. Now there are hundreds of beautifully designed decks available. Some are modern reproductions of medieval cards. Others are based on particular mythologies, or systems of magic or fantasy ideas, or are the work of well-known artists – notably Salvador Dali. Many people collect them for their own sake, rather than to use. ❧ The deck included with this kit consists of the Major Arcana, which are often used by themselves for fortune telling. Professional cartomancers use the full 78-card deck, but this complicates readings considerably, and you should certainly learn the meanings of the Major Arcana before going on to the full deck. With practice, you should be able to carry out a reading without referring back to this book.

❧ **BELOW Tarot cards are available in a variety of beautiful designs.**

❧ **FAR LEFT 16th-century tarot card – Le Monde.**

❧ **LEFT Six tarot cards by J. Blanche, Besançon.**

the major arcana

Many tarot decks bear French names for the cards, which are given here.

(R) = The meaning when the card is reversed or inverted

0 The Fool

LE MAT

Generally placed first in the Major Arcana, this is the only card not to be numbered. It may be thought of as number 0, and it is the ancestor of the Joker in contemporary playing cards. An ambiguous and subtle card, it may stand for many different actions, most of which are better avoided, such as being reckless or thoughtless or foolish or undisciplined or obsessed – all marking a difference from normal behavior. It can be a sign that one should force oneself to make the correct, though more difficult, choice. It may also symbolize the light and hedonistic side of life.

(R) = Being unable to come to a decision, or choosing wrongly.

1 The Magician

LE BATELEUR

Creativity, using one's skills to the full. Imagination, willpower. Confidence, control of oneself and others.

(R) = Indecision, weakness of will, misuse of skills or powers.

2 The High Priestess

LA PAPESSE

Knowledge and understanding, even of hidden or future events. Wise judgment and common sense. Practical. Great teaching and learning abilities.

(R) = Shallow knowledge or ignorance. Poor judgment. Conceit.

3 The Empress

L'IMPÉRATRICE

Success in any traditional female role. Domestic life in all its details. Fruitfulness and positive achievement. Feminine wiles.

(R) = Inability to maintain interest or to make decisions. Wastefulness.

4 The Emperor

L'EMPEREUR

Success in any traditional male role. Wealth, authority, strength, great spirit, great confidence. Triumph of reason over emotion. Intelligence.

(R) = Any kind of weakness or immaturity.

5 The Hierophant (or the High Priest)

LE PAPE

Ceremony. Kindness and mercy. A spiritual leader or adviser. Platonic friend and well-meaning person. Sometimes timid and inactive.

(R) = Kindness to the point of foolishness. Inability to act decisively.

6 The Lovers

L'AMOUREUX

The perfection of love, beauty, harmony. A loving relationship begins. Deep feelings and strong emotions, to which one surrenders oneself unconditionally.

(R) = A frustrated romance. Lovers separated. Unreliability.

7 The Chariot

LE CHARIOT

Trouble, upset, and change – the outcome may be good or bad. Some possibilities are success, a journey, or an escape.

(R) = Failure, defeat. Something snatched from one's grasp. Plans collapse.

8 Justice

LA JUSTICE

Balanced objectivity. Justice is done. An eventual outcome will be fair. Honor, sincerity, righteousness. Avoidance of temptation.

(R) = Any form of injustice, bias, or intolerance.

9 The Hermit

L'HERMITE

A wise counselor, prudent, self-denying and discreet. A person alone, with suggestions of desertion, unsociability, and insincerity.

(R) = Mistaken advice, imprudence, hasty action.

⑩ The Wheel of Fortune LA ROUE DE FORTUNE 	Destiny, involving great gain or great loss. A definite conclusion or completion. Unexpected events. Its meaning is tempered by adjacent cards. Ⓡ = Bad luck. Events interrupted, not completed.	**⑯ The Tower** LA MAISON-DIEU 	Change, often complete and sudden. Unexpected events. Loss of stability and setback – but not forever. Ⓡ = No change when a change would be welcome. The imprisonment of boredom.
⑪ Strength LA FORCE 	Spiritual or physical strength. Determination and courage. Success through great effort. A triumph over dangers or temptation. Ⓡ = Any form of weakness, spiritual or physical.	**⑰ The Star** L'ÉTOILE 	A card full of hope, promising opportunity, inspiration, justified success, satisfaction, pleasure, and fulfillment. Effort and achievement are balanced. Ⓡ = Disappointment. Lack of opportunity. Pessimism.
⑫ The Hanged Man LE PENDU 	Not the card of death as one might expect, but of change. All is turned upside down, and there may be a lack of progress for a while despite one's best efforts. Ⓡ = Lack of effort, lack of sacrifice.	**⑱ The Moon** LA LUNE 	The card of deception and trickery. A warning against false friends, bad influences, superficiality, insincerity, error, and other dangers. Ⓡ = Minor deceptions are noticed and avoided.
⑬ Death LA MORT 	Nor is death symbolized here. It means transformation, often in the form of an unexpected or unwelcome change. But it hints at a rebirth. Ⓡ = Stagnation, failure to change.	**⑲ The Sun** LE SOLEIL 	The card of satisfaction. Being content with one's existence, one's marriage, one's friendships. Pleasure from small and simple things. Ⓡ = Unhappiness through cancellation or delay.
⑭ Temperance LA TEMPÉRANCE 	Moderation and self-control, from which good things will come. Harmony between the material and the spiritual brings fortune and high regard. Ⓡ = Conflict, hostility, lack of harmony.	**⑳ Judgment** LE JUGEMENT 	Be prepared to repent and forgive. A time of rebirth and improvement. Legal action or personal conflicts coming to a conclusion. Development. Ⓡ = Delay, indecision. Divorce.
⑮ The Devil LE DIABLE 	Weird experience. Unexpected failure or general lack of success. Temporary inability to realize one's goals. Controversy. Ⓡ = Physical or spiritual release. Overcoming handicaps. Enlightenment.	**㉑ The World** LE MONDE 	Triumphal completion, fulfillment. The perfect result. Final change. Eternal life. Very favorable. Ⓡ = An imperfect conclusion. Failure to finish. Disappointment.

making a reading

The 22 cards of the Major Arcana are not only symbols of future events but an aid to meditation, symbolizing a journey through the human condition. ❧ Readings are normally carried out by a single diviner for a single questioner, who is usually present. The aim is generally to answer a question or to solve a problem. It does not matter whether the questioner voices this or not, as long as it is held clearly in the mind. ❧ There are variations in procedure and in the spread, or arrangement, of the cards. As few as seven cards may be used, or as many as 54 when the full deck is used; but 10 is the most usual number. ❧ Many diviners prefer to use their tarot deck only for divining and never for card games. Some insist that no one else should touch it, but others require the questioner to shuffle the deck, and generally the questioner is asked to cut it before the spread is made – all the time keeping the question or problem in mind. Traditionally, many diviners follow a few basic rules: No one should try to do a reading for themselves; once a reading is begun, it must be completed; and there should be no more than one reading for the same person, nor readings for more than three people, in a single day. ❧ As the diviner, you must remember to let your intuition guide you. Tarot reading cannot be simply a mechanical process of laying down cards and reading the meanings. Do not allow yourself to be rushed, flustered, or distracted. Make yourself comfortable: Ideally, conduct the reading in a quiet room with only the questioner sitting opposite you so that you can both concentrate more easily. ❧ The use of the full 78-card deck is not covered here. The other 56 cards influence the result by modifying the strong forecasts of the Major Arcana. This provides a more balanced reading, taking into account life's run-of-the-mill events.

❧ **ABOVE All tarot cards, not just the Major Arcana, have different meanings when they are reversed.**

❧ **RIGHT There are many different ways of spreading, or arranging, tarot cards when conducting a reading.**

the seven-card spread

Deal seven cards in a horizontal row, face up. If more than half the cards are reversed, turn all seven around. The most significant card is number 4, at the center of the row, which stands for the present obstruction if there is a problem, or the outcome if a question is being answered. Where the answer is not clear simply from reading this card, consider the others, with 1 and 2 representing the past, 3 and 5 the present, and 6 and 7 the future. If the situation is still unresolved, deal another three cards in a vertical row to the right of the last card, with the middle card level with the original row. An interpretation of these should make the answer clear.

the ten-card or celtic spread

This is in the shape of a cross with a line of four to its right. Cards must be laid down in the numbered order shown. Each card has a particular significance (see right).

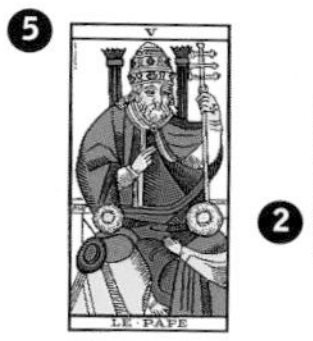

1. The present position
2. Immediate obstacles or influences
3. The questioner's goals
4. The original cause of the present difficulty
5. Recent past influences
6. Future influences
7. The questioner's present attitude
8. Environment – how the questioner influences others
9. The questioner's inner hopes and feelings
10. The final result

the I ching

THE I CHING, OR BOOK OF CHANGES, IS A VERY ANCIENT SYSTEM OF ADVICE AND PREDICTION THAT ORIGINATED IN CHINA WELL OVER 5,000 YEARS AGO. THE PHILOSOPHICAL WISDOM OF THE I CHING IS A MIXTURE OF TAOISM AND CONFUCIANISM. IT WAS NOT INTRODUCED TO THE WEST UNTIL EARLY THIS CENTURY, BUT DURING THE 1960s IT BECAME POPULAR IN THE UNITED STATES AND BRITAIN.

The book of changes consists of 64 sayings which are not only advice in their own right, but which may also be interpreted in many different ways as the answers to particular problems or questions.

In order to choose the correctly numbered answer, you will first need to construct a "hexagram" – a stack of six horizontal lines. Each of these lines may be solid or "broken." The unbroken line — is called yang. It signifies the answer yes, the positive, the active, the projective, the masculine. The broken line -- is called yin. It signifies the answer no, the negative, the passive, the receptive, and the feminine. ❧ Each hexagram consists of two "trigrams" of three lines each. There are eight possible combinations of these trigrams, and they have wide significance in Chinese philosophy, some of which are given in the table below.

generating a hexagram

There are 64 (8 x 8) possible ways to combine two trigrams into hexagrams, each of which refers to one of the 64 sections of the I Ching. Each hexagram has a complex meaning that can be interpreted as a view of the future, or as an answer to a specific question or problem. A simplified interpretation is given here. ❧ To find the hexagram that gives the answer to your own question or problem, you rely on chance. Nowadays, this is usually done by tossing three coins – some authentically Chinese ones are supplied with this fortune-telling kit. They generate one line at a time, so you have to throw them six times to provide a complete hexagram. During the tossing of the coins, the person wishing for an answer must keep the question in mind, meditating on it.

❧ BELOW **The legendary Chinese emperor Fu Hsi, with the 8 trigrams of the I Ching before him.**

❧ ABOVE **China is the home of many distinctive divination methods – from fortune cookies to Chinese astrology to I Ching coins.**

the trigrams

Sign	Name	Associated image	Attributes	Family link
☰	Ch'ien	Heaven, Sky	Strength, power	Father
☷	K'un	Earth	Fidelity, submission	Mother
☳	Chen	Thunder	Impulsiveness, provocation	Elder son
☵	K'an	Water, the Deep	Danger, flexibility	Middle son
☶	Ken	Mountain	Immobility, inevitability	Younger son
☴	Sun	Wind, Wood, Air	Subtlety, penetration	Elder daughter
☲	Li	Fire, Sun	Enlightenment, warmth	Middle daughter
☱	Tui	The Marsh, Mist, Lake	Joy, magic	Younger daughter

❧ **ABOVE The side with the least markings scores 3 (top and bottom) and that with more scores 2 (middle).**

There are two complications. First, the hexagram is built up from bottom to top. Second, there are not just yang — and yin – – lines, but also "yang becoming yin" –o– and "yin becoming yang" –x– . These last two are called "moving lines." The complete I Ching gives readings for them in each position of each hexagram. Once the lines have "moved" – that is, changed – the hexagram is a different one. Both the "before" and "after" hexagrams are relevant here and should be consulted. ❧ Toss the three coins together on to a flat surface. They have a more or less blank side, which counts as 3, and an inscribed side, which scores 2. (If you use Western coins, score 3 for heads and 2 for tails.) The only possible scores are 6, 7, 8, or 9. A score of 7 means a normal yang line — and 8 a normal yin line – – ; 6 gives a moving yin –x– and 9 a moving yang –o– . Toss the coins six times and write down the score each time, working upward. Then convert the number to a line to create your hexagram.

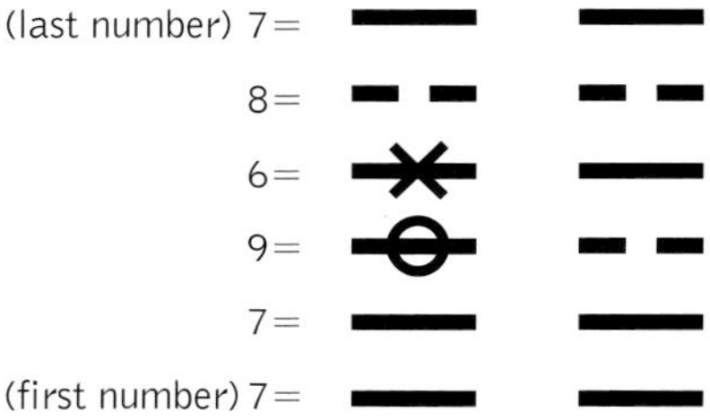

The above left is hexagram 18. The hexagram has one moving yin line and one moving yang line, so that it turns into hexagram 38, as shown on the right. There is no room here to give the extra symbolism of the moving lines, but the interpretations of hexagrams 18 and 38 can be looked up and compared.

1 Yang

You will achieve your objectives through hard work and patience. Plan well. Avoid conflict and strain.

2 Yin

Be cautious and modest in your desires. Allow those in charge to make decisions for you.

3 Growing Pains

Learn to advance slowly. Do not set your sights too high. Accept help.

4 Youthful Ignorance

Be prepared to learn. Follow the advice of those more experienced.

5 Waiting

Avoid danger by waiting. Your chance will come once the danger is past.

6 Conflict

Some strife is inevitable. Be flexible, keep a low profile, and wait for better times.

7 Soldiers

Battle is almost inevitable. Be flexible, keep a low profile, and wait for better times.

8 Seeking Union

Make the most of peaceful times. Cooperate sincerely with others.

9 Minor Restraint

Be prudent and cautious during difficult times. Seek to make the best of the circumstances.

10 Treading

Be honest and resolute, without hesitation or doubt, or you may fall.

11 Peace

Be generous to others during yo good times, and it will benefit yo Action is called for.

12 Disjunction

Plan for the future and accept standstill or small gains for the present.

13 Society

Better times will come eventuall Cooperate and you will achieve success.

14 Wealth

By learning and training you wi improve your chances. Avoid trying to impress.

15 Modesty

Only if you are humble and modest will others help you. Success will come.

16 Enthusiasm

Infect others with your enthusiasm, but try to avoid arrogance.

17 Following

For the moment, let others take the lead. Once they have guided you to safety, you may be able to command.

18 Fixing

Work hard at righting a wrong. Be energetic and scrupulous.

19 Conduct

Assertiveness has gained you you current position, but now you ca afford to be magnanimous.

20 Contemplation

You must be perceptive and not too trusting. Think and move but do not hesitate.

the meanings of hexagrams

21
Biting Through
䷔

Blow your own trumpet to counter the comments and small jealousies of others.

22
Beauty
䷕

Adopt attractive, showy façade as long as it helps. Then abandon it.

23
Collapse
䷖

Odds are against you, so prepare for losses and begin planning for the future.

24
Returning
䷗

Learn to react to the changing seasons. Renew your energy. Do not force changes through at the wrong time.

25
The Simple
䷘

Wait for your time to come. Be honest, accept your limitations.

26
Major Restraint
䷙

Your potential is great, but you must show restraint now. Work hard and wait for your chance.

27
Nourishment
䷚

Charge your energies patiently, and you will be strong when the time comes for action.

28
Greatness in Excess
䷛

Although change is coming, if you truly know your strengths and weaknesses, you will survive.

29
The Deep
䷜

Do not move now. Danger threatens, but wait for guidance.

30
Fire
䷝

Use your intellect and your powers of logic, but harness them both.

31
Tension
䷞

Turn aside from envy, because those who seem more successful have more to lose.

32
Continuity
䷟

Perseverance and a casual acceptance will bring results. Haste will not.

33
Retreat
䷠

Be watchful of tricksters. Be prepared to use guile yourself.

34
Great Strength
䷡

Do not boast or bluster. You may have to take strong action to maintain your position.

35
Advance
䷢

Good fortune and progress are yours, but you must be honest and above suspicion in all things.

36
Darkening of the Light
䷣

Difficult times approach. Wait them out with good grace and conditions will improve.

37
The Family
䷤

Concentrate on your immediate surroundings, solving problems or enhancing harmony.

38
Neutrality
䷥

Avoid dogmatism, even if you are right. Be flexible and mend fences.

39
Difficulty
䷦

Complaint will not solve problems. Adapt or ask for help.

40
Release
䷧

Rid yourself of dead weight. A situation is coming to a head.

41
Decrease
䷨

When you achieve success or riches, remember those who have helped you.

42
Increase
䷩

Make the most of good opportunities; do not expect them to last.

43
Breakthrough
䷪

Make plans as an insurance against troubles. Guard against evil.

44
Temptation
䷫

Beware of harmful influence, especially from the strong. Keep calm and influence others.

45
Accord
䷬

Opposition is coming. Either keep a low profile or find allies for the fight.

46
Pushing Upward
䷭

Keep growing, like a seed. Do not falter and you will reach your goal eventually.

47
Repression
䷮

During hard times have confidence in yourself. Keep calm and do your best.

48
The Well
䷯

Persevere, even if the job is boring. Make sure you get the credit.

49
Revolution
䷰

You can make yourself appear better to others, but only if you choose your moment well.

50
The Cauldron
䷱

Be cautious and check details. Ignore small mishaps but concentrate on preventing large ones.

51
The Thunderclap
䷲

Keep your spirits up during stormy weather and be ready to move when the storm is over.

52
Keeping Still
䷳

A time for pausing and recuperation. Do not be too eager to rush onward.

53
Procession
䷴

Slow progress is possible, so be patient. Do not expect too much.

54
The Marrying Maiden
䷵

Learn to be satisfied with what is available. Wait for more to be offered.

55
Abundance
䷶

If you can keep up your spirits, even the worst trouble will be lessened.

56
The Stranger
䷷

Be particular about your own appearance and cautious as to your associates.

57
The Penetration of the Wind
䷸

If you can be reasonable, you will be accepted. Find the easiest course.

58
Pleasure
䷹

If you can find inner contentment, others will notice and react well.

59
Dispersion
䷺

Be reasonable in your demands but do not let your ideas or plans be dissolved away.

60
Restraint
䷻

Be cautious, accept limitations, and follow the rules, and you will succeed.

61
Understanding
䷼

Be aware of warning signs and act upon them. In this way you will survive the storm.

62
Smallness in Excess
䷽

Curb your ambitions and be cautious. However weak your position, you will make gains.

63
Completion
䷾

Be careful not to lose all your gains. Look to the future with optimism.

64
Almost There
䷿

Experience will tell you when to move forward. Be wise and cautious.

RUNES

THE RUNES USED FOR DIVINATION ARE DERIVED FROM A RUNIC ALPHABET THAT WAS CURRENT ACROSS MUCH OF EUROPE FROM PRE-CHRISTIAN TIMES UNTIL THE 13TH CENTURY. THE WORD COMES FROM RUNA, THE GOTHIC (ANCIENT GERMANIC) TERM FOR A MYSTERY OR SOMETHING KEPT SECRET. THE LETTER SHAPES OF THE RUNIC ALPHABET ARE COMPOSED OF STRAIGHT LINES, BECAUSE THEY WERE MEANT TO BE CARVED INTO STONE, AND IT IS MUCH EASIER TO CHISEL STRAIGHT LINES THAN CURVES.

There are suggestions that, even in the earliest times, runes were used for divination as well as for written communication – now, of course, they are used purely for divination purposes.

It is claimed that the alphabet was originally a gift to mankind from Odin, the king of the Norse gods. It is often known as the futhork alphabet, after the names of the first six letters. ❧ Runes coexisted with the Roman alphabet but, as time went on, were used more for divination and as a secret language in which spells and folk remedies could be written. The last of the rune masters lived in Iceland about 300 years ago, then the system was forgotten until recently. From the late 1970s to the present date, the use of runes for divination purposes has made a dramatic comeback. ❧ The usual method is to use runestones: small stones each inscribed with a single rune. The standard set has 25 stones: 24 with symbols and one blank, this last being a modern invention.

❧ LEFT **Runes have a long tradition of magic associated with them, and diviners may use a variety of symbolic items when conducting a reading.**

Selecting runestones

You can buy a set of runestones or make them yourself. Almost any material can be used – some writers have allowed **cardboard** or **thick paper** – but the feel of the stones is an important factor in their use. Best are **flat pebbles** or small tablets of **wood**. You could also inscribe runes on pieces of **modeling clay** and fire them. You may like to observe certain archaic rituals in the making of a set of runes, which will give you more confidence in their fortune telling qualities.

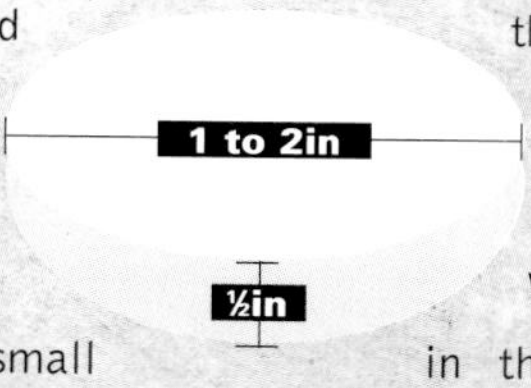

❧ ABOVE **Wood, cardboard, and even thick paper can be used to make runestones.**

❧ **BELOW You may prefer to mark the top of the runestone with a dot.**

Cut the wood from a special tree, for example a small branch from an ancient oak. First, be sure to ask the tree itself for permission, and pay by leaving a small silver coin lodged in a crack in the bark. If you use pebbles, gather them at an auspicious time, such as midnight during a waning moon. ❧ Ideally, the runestones should vary in size and shape. They should be roughly oval in outline, 1–2 inches long and perhaps ½ inch thick. You can cut the letters into wood with any sharp knife, or burn them in with a heated metal spike or woodburning tool. With pebbles, it is easiest to paint the letters on, but for the most elegant results use a fine grinding or engraving tool. ❧ Sixteen of the runes look different when upside down, while the other nine are symmetrical. Since the meanings of the runes differ depending on whether the runestone is reversed or not, some users mark the upper end of each runestone with a dot. ❧ It is customary to keep runestones in a small drawstring bag, which must be large enough for the runestones to be mixed randomly.

❧ **RIGHT Pay for wood to make runestones by placing a silver coin in the bark of the tree; if you use pebbles, gather by moonlight; keep your runestones in a drawstring bag.**

preparation

All methods of divination with runes begin with achieving the correct mood. This spiritual aspect is extremely important. It may be that you should choose a suitable time of day, or meditate for a few minutes, or perhaps light a candle or incense stick. You must compose yourself quietly and focus on your need for consulting the runes. ❧ On the whole, it is better to decide clearly in your mind what issue or problem you are concerned with, rather than asking a specific question. You can do this whether the issue affects you or whether you are obtaining guidance for somebody else – and the other person need not be present. Sometimes the runes will offer an answer which does not seem to fit, which may mean that there is another, more significant issue to which the answer is referring. ❧ If you are uncertain whether or not to consult the runes, or whether to consult them on behalf of somebody else whom you have not asked, you may ask the runes this question. Take one rune from the bag for the answer: If it comes out the right way up, the answer is yes; if it is reversed or inverted, the answer is no.

YES

NO

There are several methods of consulting the runes. The simplest is to reach into the bag and remove three runes without looking at them. Only then should you turn over all three and see what they have to say.

Rune meanings

R = The meaning when the runestone is reversed or inverted

Feohg
Wealth, property, financial gain, status, security
R Loss

Ur
Physical strength or skill, masculinity, determination
R Physical or metaphorical weakness, missed opportunities

Thorn
Protection, defense, caution, patience
R Wrong decision, over-caution

Os
Authority, advice, parents
R Problems with authority figures

Rad
Change, movement, a journey, progress
R Travel problems, unhelpful changes

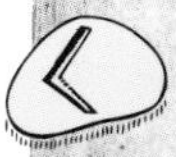

Ken
Warmth, celebration, love, success
R Lack of warmth or direction

Gyfu
A gift, opportunity, partnership, teamwork
R Loss, illegality, inability to perform a task

Wyn
Joy, a water connection, luck
R Depression, martyrdom

Hagal
Sudden change, more often bad than good, disruption
R Delay and disruption, even disaster

Nyd
Basic needs, a warning to be patient, self-preservation
R Emotional tension

Is
Standstill, plans or emotions frozen, a warning not to press on
R The same but even more so, coldness, illness

Ger
Ending and renewal, future growth
R The same

Eoh
Flexibility, avoiding problems
R Indecision, regression

Peorth
Mystery, the not-yet-known, psychic links
R Fear and disappointment

Eolhs
Creativity, artistry, culture
R A lack of these

Sygel
Wholeness, life force, rest, recovery
R The same, but perhaps overused

Tir
Victory through energy and heroism, passion
R Weakness, a broken love affair

Beorc
Growth and fertility, beginnings, good news
R Barrenness, illness, delay

Eow
Transportation, animals, changes, newcomers
R Problems with any of these

Man
A male authority figure, a warning to consult an expert before proceeding
R Trouble with authority figures

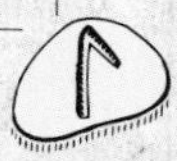

Lagu
Feminine intuition, the fluidity of change, fertility
R Paranoia, blood, serious problems

Ing
Fertility, family, good results
R Lack of productivity, restriction

Daeg
Clarity, anything obvious, success, improvement
R The same

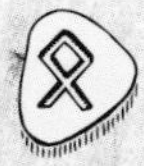

Ethel
Inheritance, the home, money matters
R Problems with any of these

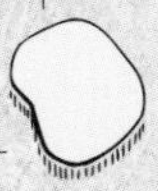

blank
Fate or destiny, things unknown – meaning affected by adjacent runes

Another reading system uses 13 runes. Take all 25 out of their bag, lay them face down, and move them around at random. Then select 13 and, still without looking at their faces, arrange 12 of them as if on a clock face, starting at 9 o'clock and going counterclockwise. The thirteenth goes in the center. Now turn them all over. Their positions – still counting from 9 o'clock – refer to different things, as listed on the right. For this type of reading, "upright" means with the tops of the runes closest to the center of the circle.

positions

1 = 9 o'clock, then count counterclockwise
13 = center

1 Personality
2 Material wealth
3 Family
4 Home
5 Self-expression
6 Health and environment
7 Love and marriage
8 Inheritance
9 Education
10 Job, status
11 Pleasures, friendship
12 Psychic feelings
13 The questioner

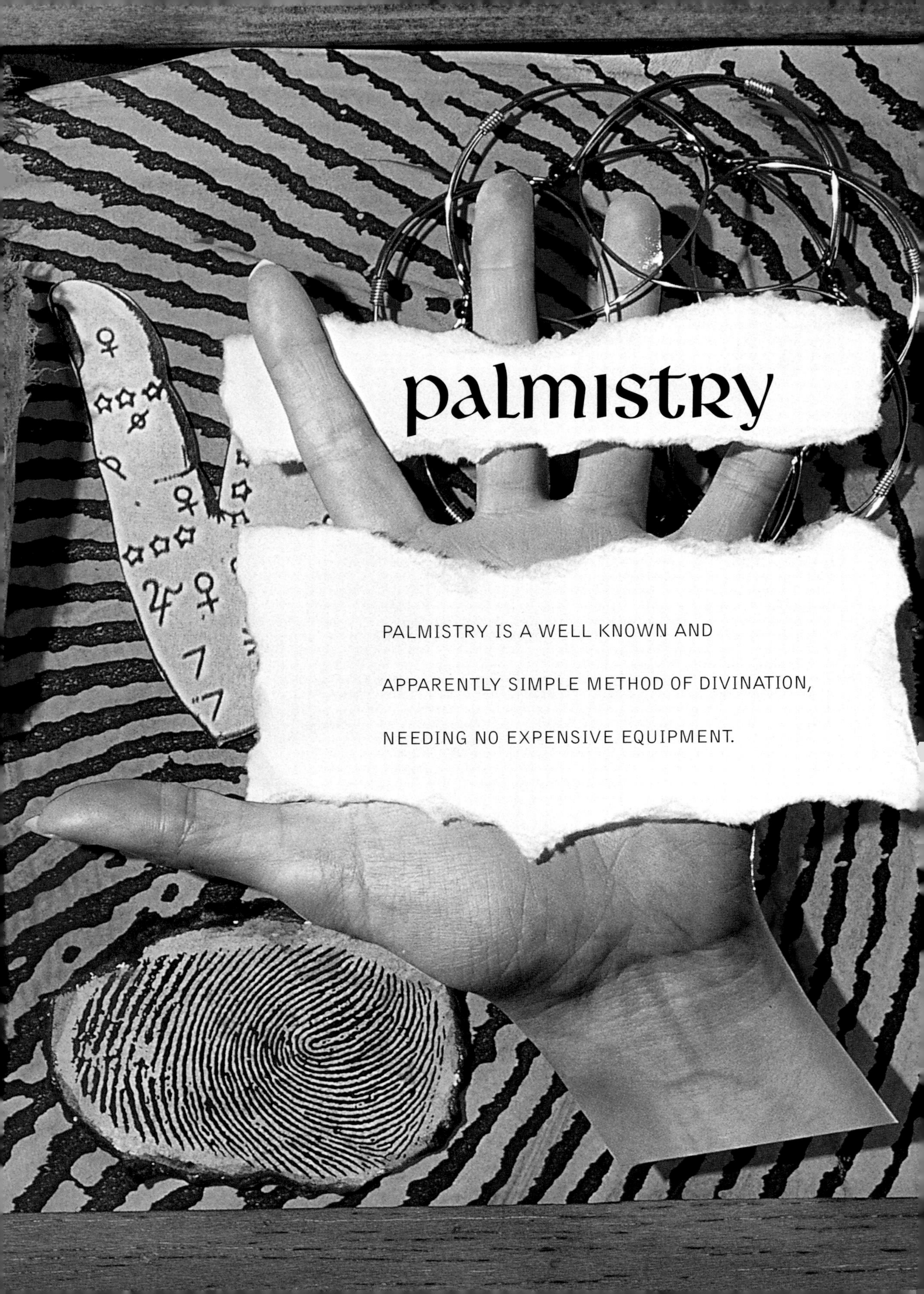

palmistry

PALMISTRY IS A WELL KNOWN AND APPARENTLY SIMPLE METHOD OF DIVINATION, NEEDING NO EXPENSIVE EQUIPMENT.

Most people think that a quick look at the palm is all that is needed to reveal the subject's whole fortune, from their general character traits to their future loves and even their date of death.

Yet this is not so. Palmistry – or chiromancy, to give its formal name – is concerned with the whole hand, not simply the palm, and is limited in the information it can provide. ❧ The origins of palmistry date back to at least 3200 B.C., when it was first recorded in China. Unlike some other methods of divination, it was not discovered separately by different cultures but seems to have spread gradually from China to the Middle East and to ancient Greece by 340 B.C., when it began to be mentioned in Greek philosophical writings. From there it spread to Rome, and thence throughout Western Europe. Medieval scientists and mystics developed theories of its significance. ❧ There are two ways of reading hands. The first is to examine the subject's whole hand, noting its shape, to feel it, look at the nails, consider the thumb, and then finally read the lines on the palm and elsewhere and to offer the subject some useful pointers on their ideal job, prospects of good health, and chances of a successful marriage, all in general rather than exact terms. The second is to ignore the formal rules for reading hands, and use the touching of the subject's hand as the starting point for a psychic reading, which may well provide much more detailed prophecies based on intuition. Many palmists combine both approaches. ❧ Psychic ability cannot be taught or even explained, so only the basic rules for reading hands will be described here.

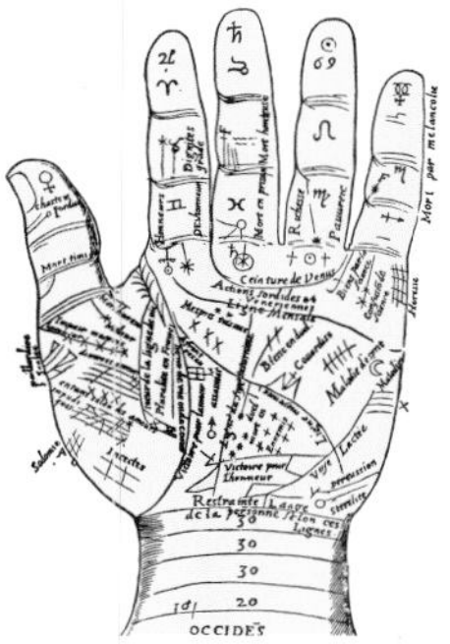

❧ **ABOVE** **17th-century French engraving showing the planetary and zodiacal areas of influence.**

❧ **LEFT** **Palm reading is traditionally associated with gypsies, as shown in this 19th-century illustration.**

hand shapes

Both hands must be examined. In a right-handed person, the right hand shows changes, successes, and future events, while the left shows the natural or original hand, as it was at birth, demonstrating potential and no more. It is the other way around for left-handed people. Begin your reading with the general hand shape. Here are four different hand shapes, each denoting specific aptitudes:

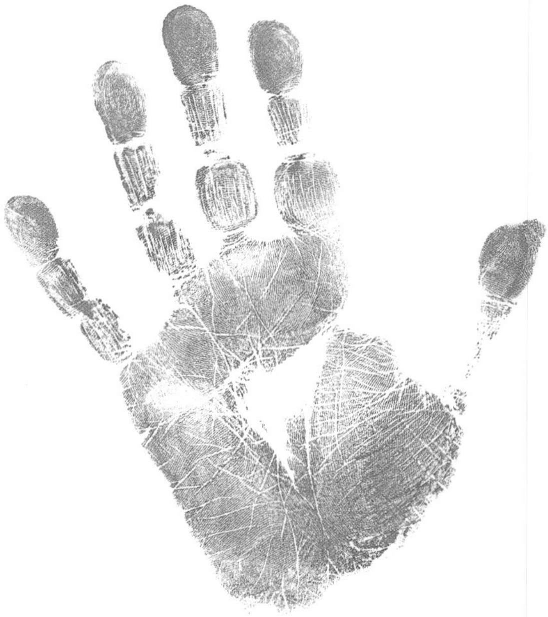

The **intuitive** hand, with short fingers and a long palm, belongs to an individualist who eschews theory and flits between interests, but who may be very quick and intelligent.

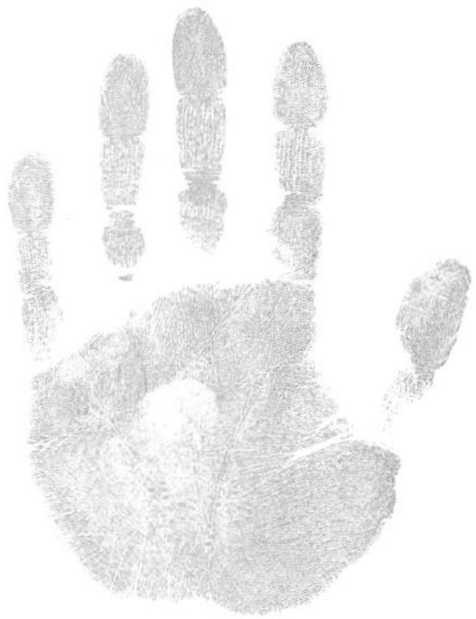

The **intellectual** hand has long fingers and a short palm; it denotes a person who thinks deeply and clearly, and who is capable of planning and of taking control.

The **sensitive** hand, with both the palm and the fingers being long, indicates an artistic person strongly influenced by emotions and imagination, and perhaps hampered by fluctuations of mood and a tendency to self-regard.

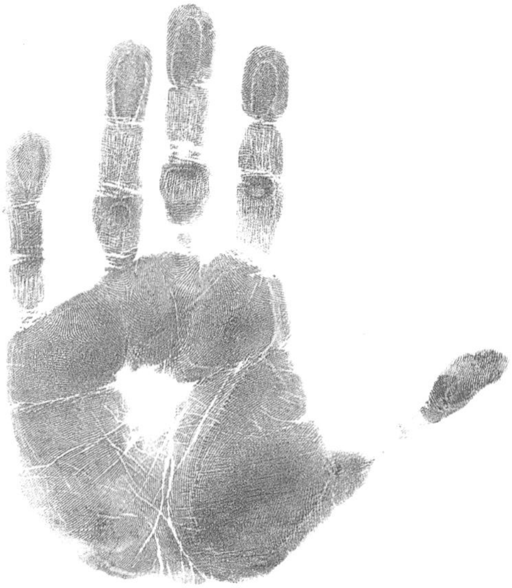

The **practical** hand, with the palm and fingers both short and broad, indicates an artisan who enjoys being a subordinate, who works hard, and who has few intellectual or artistic pretensions.

Finger shape, too, is important: Whether each finger is straight or bent, spatulate (with a flattened tip), conical, square, or pointed, and whether these shapes match or are mixed, the relative sizes of the mounts between the joints, and even whether the fingers tend to be very close or slightly separated. Spatulate fingertips indicate great originality, and separated fingers a free-thinking individual. ❧ The general feel of the hands, their skin texture and tightness, can suggest personality, from the great resolution of those with hard hands to the laziness and moodiness of those with flabby hands. ❧ The thumb is examined and assessed separately. If it is in proportion to the fingers, health, wealth, and happiness are assured. A shorter thumb means that less success will come, even from greater efforts; a longer one suggest a greater potential but perhaps a lack of achievement. Its general shape is indicative of personality type, while its flexibility and relative joint lengths point to mental balance. ❧ The shape of fingernails and thumbnails also has meaning:

nail shapes

Wedge	Oversensitive
Bulbous	Inclined to be jealous
Short	Rational, with scientific leanings
Short and broad	Too critical, uncontrolled
Wide	Liable to be blunt and undiplomatic
Long, oval	Courteous and thoughtful
Squarish	Remote, unemotional
Long and broad	Good judgment
Tilted out	Talented
Fluted	Nervous
Ridged	Liable to poor health

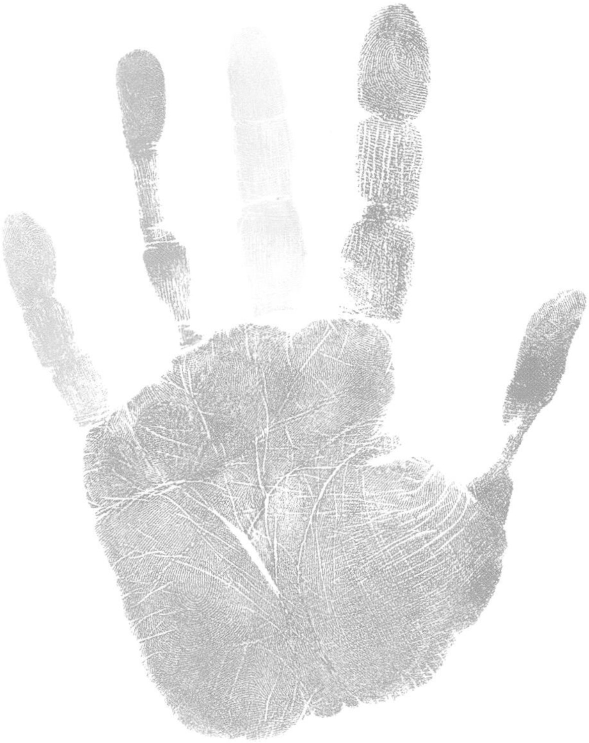

❧ LEFT **This composite hand demonstrates a variety of finger shapes: (from left to right) conical, bent, short, straight and pointed.**

RIGHT The major palm lines and mounts that are used in palmistry

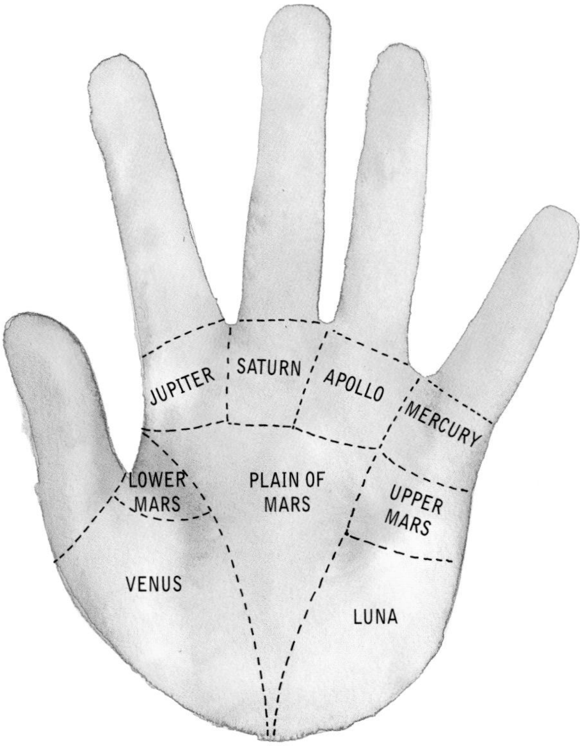

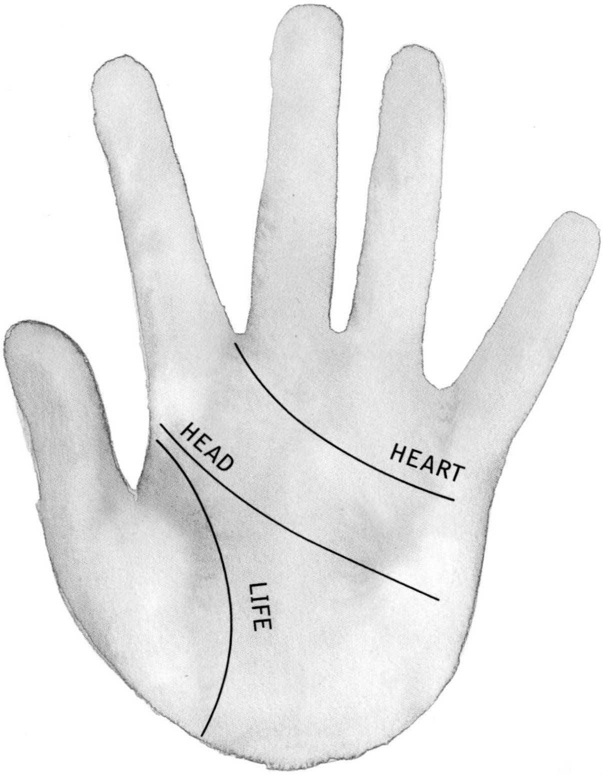

lines

Lines are many and varied, not all being present in everyone. To begin with, ignore the mass of small lines and learn to identify the three major lines: the Heart line, the Head line, and the Life line, as illustrated below left.

❧ The **Heart** line controls emotions; from it the subject's general quality of love life and capacity for feelings may be found. For example, a firm line, clear for its whole length, means a person who is generous, warm-hearted, and completely faithful. If the Heart line is firmer than the Head line, the heart will be bound to rule the head – and vice versa. Most Heart lines begin at the base of the index finger; where it begins between the first two fingers, its possessor will be extremely sensual and caring, but if it begins below the second finger, an uncaring sensuality is denoted. Branches in the line indicate a flirt, while breaks or chains suggest an unfaithful person. A lightly marked line means a lack of emotion and no love or romance.

❧ The **Head** line controls the intellect – the degree of rationality and intelligence. In the most practical of people, it goes straight across the palm. Where it slopes down toward the mount of Luna, the person tends to be both sensitive and imaginative; and where it slopes up toward the Heart line, it indicates good business sense. A clear, deep Head line means commitment and concentration on the matter at hand; breaks or chains suggest a diminution of such power.

❧ The **Life** line represents the subject's record of health and longevity. On the whole, the longer and more clearly defined this line, the longer you will live and the healthier you will be – but it is important to realize that it does not show the date of your death, as popularly supposed. Breaks indicate radical changes to your life, or perhaps serious illnesses, though not necessarily a short life. If the Life line crosses the Head line, an ambitious life is likely. Branches tend to mean success. Cross lines, chains, or tiny islands along the line are usually a sign of periods of poor health.

mounts

The palm of the hand also has seven "mounts", as illustrated top left. These are easily identified, even though they are often apparent not as mounts but as flat or hollowed areas. Whichever of the mounts is the most noticeable, most raised, gives a key to the subject's personality.

mounts

Jupiter	Ambition, social advancement; if two lines form a cross on this mount, it indicates a happy marriage
Saturn	Reserved, cautious, solitary, probably unmarried
Apollo	Successful, artistic, practical, healthy
Mercury	Hopeful, managerial, even criminal
Luna	Imaginative, intuitive, creative, or just a dreamer
Venus	Loving, passionate, sympathetic, perhaps too sensual and self-indulgent
Mars	If the lower mount is more noticeable, the person will fight for any just cause; if the upper is more noticeable, the person is more defensive and persistent; a well-developed plain means the subject is short-tempered

There are many minor lines, some difficult to distinguish or not always present. Their influence upon the subject's life is less and will always be overshadowed by the major factors of the hand's general appearance, the three main lines, and the mounts.

WESTERN ASTROLOGY

MOST PEOPLE READ THEIR "STARS" IN THE NEWSPAPER, BUT FOR A MORE ACCURATE PREDICTION, YOU HAVE TO CAST A PROPER HOROSCOPE OR BIRTH CHART SHOWING THE EXACT POSITIONS OF THE CONSTELLATIONS AND PLANETS VISIBLE AT THE TIME AND PLACE OF YOUR BIRTH.

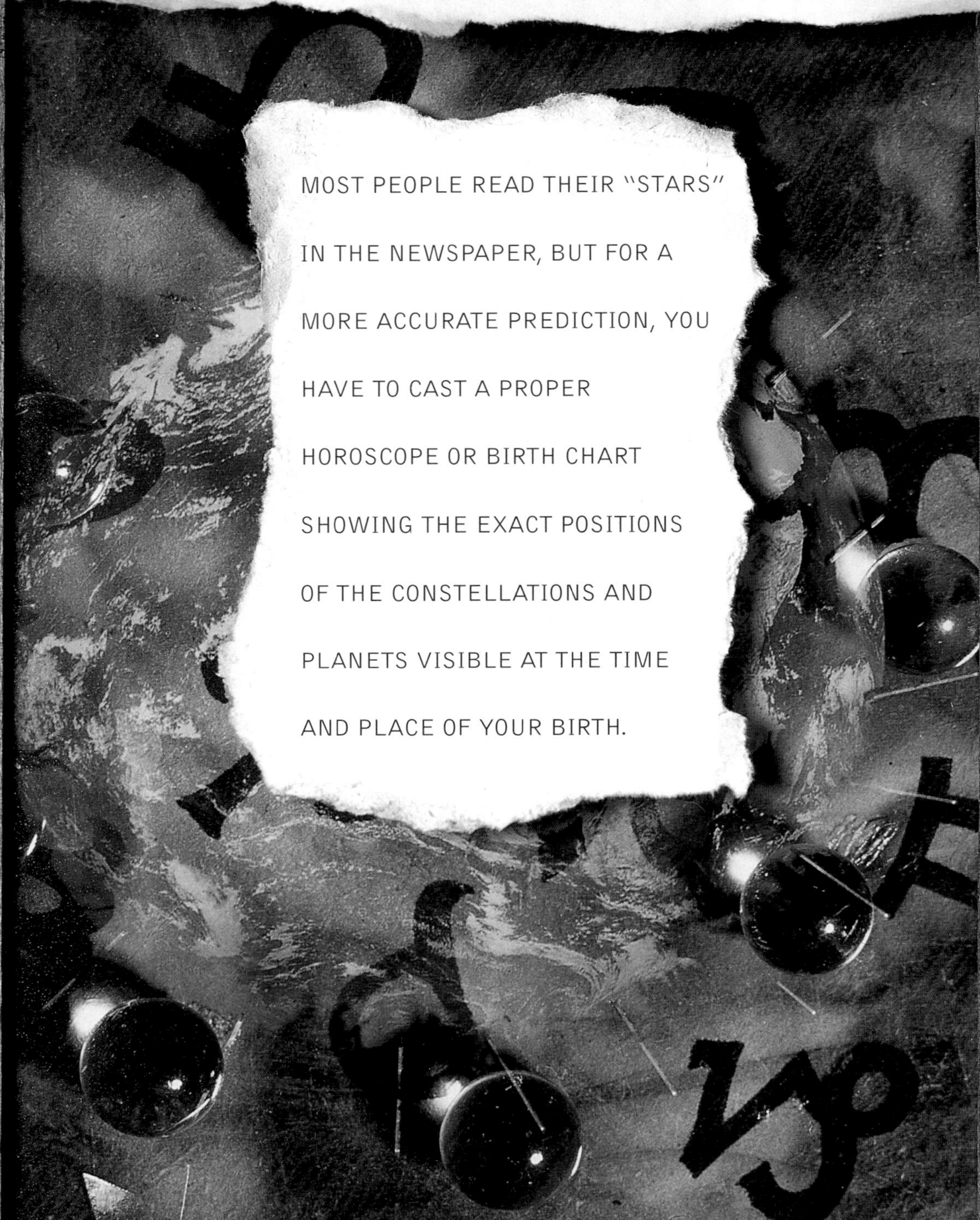

astrological terms

A full birth chart or horoscope is beyond the scope of this book, but here is a useful list of astrological terms and a chart of the romantic compatibility of people with various star signs.

AIR One of the four elements or triplicities.

AQUARIUS The Water Carrier, the eleventh sign of the Zodiac, covering those born between January 21 and February 19. Ruled by Uranus. There are two distinct types: the shy and sensitive ones and the lively exhibitionists. Generally they are intelligent and logical, with frank, open personalities.

ARIES The Ram, the first sign of the Zodiac, covering those born between March 21 and April 20. Ruled by Mars. An Aries may be a strong leader, adventurous, and full of energy, but liable to be impatient and immoderate. They are candid and generous friends and may be passionate partners.

ASCENDANT The sign and degree of the Zodiac which is rising on the eastern horizon at the place and time of birth. It also forms the cusp of the first house on a birth chart.

ASPECT Angles formed between planets on a birth chart.

ASTROLOGY The study of the effects that the positions of the Sun, Moon, and planets have on human beings, both at their time of birth and through the rest of their lives. It is at least 5,000 years old, and was probably the first science studied by mankind. The Babylonians, Greeks, Chinese, and Arabs all made major contributions to its development. It was often frowned on by Christians and almost disappeared from Europe during the Dark Ages. In the seventeenth century, after a gradual revival of interest, astronomy split away from astrology. Today astrology is most widely encountered as predictions in newspapers and magazines, though there is also interest in the preparation of birth charts.

BIRTH CHART (or horoscope) A schematic diagram of the sky as it was at the minute when, and seen from the place where, a particular event occurred. Most frequently, this is a birth, though it may be another personal event such as a marriage or perhaps the launch of a new enterprise. Calculating your birth chart used to be a difficult mathematical procedure involving the use of ephemeris tables and was best left to an expert, but modern computer software has made it easy.

CANCER The Crab, the fourth sign of the Zodiac, covering those born between June 22 and July 22. Ruled by the Moon – Americans refer to Cancerians as "Moon Children." They tend to be family-based people, who prefer home life, or even their own company. Cancerians are usually artistic, reserved, loyal, and sympathetic.

CAPRICORN The Goat, the tenth sign of the Zodiac, covering those born between December 23 and January 20. Ruled by Saturn. Capricornians are usually stable and serious personalities, honest, self-disciplined, and not easily bored. They may also be somewhat pessimistic and reserved.

CONJUNCTION An aspect when two planets are within 8° of each other, thus reinforcing each other.

CUSP The line that divides two houses or two signs of the Zodiac.

DESCENDANT That sign and degree of the Zodiac which is setting on the western horizon at the time and place of birth.

EARTH One of the four elements or triplicities.

ABOVE 16th-century Turkish depiction of the zodiacal sign of Cancer.

ECLIPTIC The apparent path of the Sun through the sky.

ELECTIONAL ASTROLOGY Using astrology to select a lucky birth date for a project or a business venture.

ELEMENTS The four elements of astrology are earth, air, fire, and water, each relating to three zodiacal signs:

Earth	Air	Fire	Water
Taurus	Gemini	Aries	Cancer
Virgo	Libra	Leo	Scorpio
Capricorn	Aquarius	Sagittarius	Pisces

FIRE One of the four elements or triplicities.

GEMINI The Twins, the third sign of the Zodiac, covering those born between May 21 and June 21. Ruled by Mercury. Geminians tend to have a dual nature, being complex and versatile, yet also flighty and fickle. When they persevere, they can be hugely successful in whatever they do, though usually they move on to a new interest first.

GLYPH The symbol used for a sign of the Zodiac or a planet.

ABOVE Pisces – from an English Psalter manuscript, c. 1170.

GREENWICH MERIDIAN The base line of 0° running through Greenwich Observatory, London, from which lines of longitude are calculated toward the east and west.

HOROSCOPE See Birth chart.

HOUSES The twelve slices into which the birth chart is divided, moving counterclockwise from the ascendant. Each house is concerned with a particular area of your life for prediction purposes:

1. Self
2. Possessions
3. Communications
4. Domestic life
5. Leisure
6. Health and daily work
7. Personal relationships
8. Sharing
9. Travel
10. Career
11. Friendships
12. Inner feelings

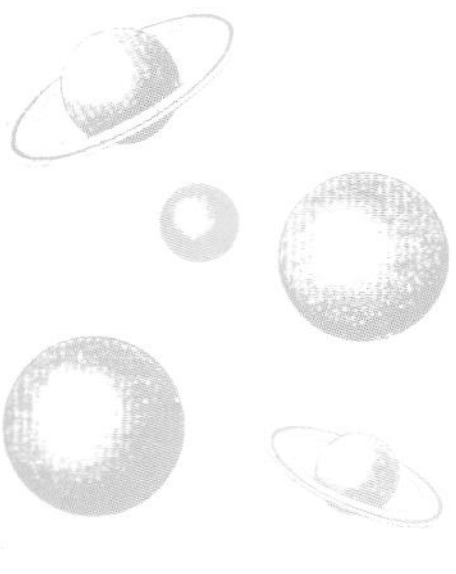

ABOVE The position of the planets and stars form the basis of horoscopes.

IMUM COELI (pronounced eye-mum see-lie) The base or nadir of heaven on the birth chart, shown at the bottom or northernmost point (on northern hemisphere charts). Usually abbreviated to IC.

LEO The Lion, the fifth sign of the Zodiac, covering those born between July 23 and August 22. Ruled by the Sun. Leos are most often dominant extroverts, honest and self-confident. Sometimes, however, these many fine qualities become so exaggerated that they turn into arrogance, jealousy, and bad temper.

LIBRA The Scales, the seventh sign of the Zodiac, covering those born between September 23 and October 22. Ruled by Venus. Being a Libran is all about balance: They are most often civilized and mellow personalities, kind, diplomatic, and with artistic leanings. They are sometimes too moderate, too attracted to the opposite sex to be monogamous, and too sure of the truth to accept challenges to their opinions.

MEDIUM COELI The mid-heaven or zenith on the birth chart, shown at the top or southernmost point (for southern hemisphere charts). Usually abbreviated to MC.

OPPOSITION The aspect of two planets being opposite each other across the birth chart, in other words at 180°.

PISCES The Fish, the twelfth sign of the Zodiac, covering those born between February 20 and March 20. Ruled by Neptune. Pisceans tend to be gentle, easily led people, who are friendly, compassionate, and generally very popular. Their faults are a lack of assertiveness, a dislike of discipline, and a general weakness of will.

PLANETS Astrologically speaking, this refers to the Sun, the Moon (neither of which is actually a planet, of course), Mercury, Venus, Mars, Jupiter, Saturn, Uranus, Neptune, and Pluto. Each is ascribed certain characteristics, which affect the signs of the Zodiac while it transits that constellation, either at birth or at a future time for which a prediction is being made (the latter is sometimes called a "progressed chart").

RISING PLANET Any planet within 8° of the ascendant, its effect on the interpretation being increased by its proximity. Also known as a strong planet.

SAGITTARIUS The Archer, the ninth sign of the Zodiac, covering those born between November 23 and December 22. Ruled by Jupiter. Sagittarians are very positive, honest, and sincere, being full of energy, enterprise, and ambition. They may be fickle, though only in response to a sincere change of heart.

SCORPIO The Scorpion, the eighth sign of the Zodiac, covering those born between October 23 and November 22. Ruled by Pluto. Scorpians are among the most intense and powerful of characters. They may seem magnetic, dynamic, and full of energy for work and play. But if they fail to control this energy or to channel it properly, they can become angry, blunt, unforgiving, and very difficult to live or work with.

SEXTILE An aspect when planets are 60° apart from each other.

SIDEREAL TIME Star time, used for astrology and astronomy, which is based on the time it takes a star that is overhead one night to be overhead again. It is longer than our normal solar time by 10 seconds per hour.

SUN-SIGN ASTROLOGY A crude, highly simplified form of astrology, taking account only of your "sun sign" – that is, Zodiac sign.

SYNASTRY A comparison of birth charts.

TAURUS The Bull, the second sign of the Zodiac, covering those born between April 21 and May 20. Ruled by Venus. Taureans tend to be solid, practical, and well-balanced. They are faithful in love and industrious at work. They may be rather obstinate or get stuck in a rut.

TRINE An aspect in which planets are 120° apart from each other.

TRIPLICITIES A group of three signs of the Zodiac linked to each of the four elements.

VIRGO The Virgin, the sixth sign of the Zodiac, covering those born between August 23 and September 22. Ruled by Mercury. Virgos are often intelligent and refined, fastidious, and creative. Being more reserved than other star signs, they tend to have few friends, rarely letting others know them well. They can appear emotionally cold, which is often just a façade for their lack of confidence.

WATER One of the elements or triplicities.

ZODIAC A relatively narrow band of stars, about 18° wide, circling the Earth, against which the Sun, Moon, and planets appear to move. It is divided into twelve segments, the signs of the Zodiac, named after the constellations which more or less occupy each segment. It was developed as a concept some 5,000 years ago.

compatibility in love

5 = most compatible, 1 = least compatible

FEMALE \ MALE	Aries	Taurus	Gemini	Cancer	Leo	Virgo	Libra	Scorpio	Sagittarius	Capricorn	Aquarius	Pisces
Aries	1	2	1	3	5	1	3	2	3	2	1	1
Taurus	2	3	1	3	1	3	2	3	1	5	1	2
Gemini	2	1	3	2	2	1	5	2	3	2	3	1
Cancer	1	3	1	3	1	2	2	5	2	2	1	3
Leo	2	1	2	1	3	2	2	3	5	2	3	1
Virgo	1	3	1	1	3	2	2	1	1	5	2	3
Libra	2	2	5	1	3	1	2	2	1	2	3	2
Scorpio	3	3	1	3	2	1	1	3	1	2	1	5
Sagittarius	2	1	1	1	3	1	2	1	5	1	3	1
Capricorn	2	3	1	1	2	5	2	2	1	2	1	2
Aquarius	1	1	3	1	3	2	3	1	2	1	5	1
Pisces	3	2	1	5	1	3	2	3	1	2	1	3

chinese astrology

THIS BOOK IS BEING WRITTEN IN THE YEAR OF THE PIG, AND IT WILL BE PUBLISHED IN THE YEAR OF THE RAT. TEN OR FIFTEEN YEARS AGO, THAT STATEMENT WOULD NOT HAVE BEEN UNDERSTOOD BY MOST PEOPLE IN THE UNITED STATES OR BRITAIN.

Since then, the Chinese astrological system of animal years has been highly publicized, and now nearly everyone has heard of it, through books, magazine features, and Chinese New Year celebrations.

There are twelve animal year signs, following each other in a regular cycle: The year of the Pig fell in 1995, and before that in 1983 and 1971. The next year of the Pig will be 2007. ❧ Chinese astrological years do not correspond exactly to our calendar years because they are based on the lunar cycle. The Chinese New Year can fall on any day from late January to late February in the Western calendar. ❧ We have used the traditional Chinese animal signs in this book but note that in some countries, such as Korea and Tibet, the names can differ slightly. The twelve animals in the cycle are, in order, the Rat, the Ox (or Buffalo), the Tiger, the Rabbit (or Cat or Hare), the Dragon, the Snake, the Horse, the Goat, the Monkey, the Rooster (or Cockerel), the Dog, and the Pig (or Boar). There is no connection between Chinese astrology and Western astrology, and the twelve animals have nothing to do with our twelve signs of the Zodiac. ❧ The basis of the Chinese animal system is that people born in a particular year are likely to possess particular traits of personality. So a person born in 1960 (the year of the Rat) will be different from a person born in 1959 (the year of the Pig) or 1961 (the year of the Ox), but will tend to have some similarities with a person born in 1948 or 1972 (also years of the Rat). This is an oversimplification of the system; in fact, there are subtle differences between people born in different years that have the same sign. ❧ The animal signs are the best known feature of Chinese astrology, but they are only a small and relatively unimportant part of a very complex system of divination.

A professional Chinese astrologer will use your month, day, and hour of birth to cast a horoscope that will give a much more accurate assessment of your fortunes. ❧ Remember that predictions of the future by Chinese astrology are only warnings of what may happen to you. Nothing is inevitable: You can change any prediction for your future by your own willpower.

❧ ABOVE **Divination has been an important part of daily life in China since ancient times.**

❧ LEFT **Each astrological year is associated with a particular animal, such as the monkey.**

the Rat

Feb 5, 1924–Jan 24, 1925	Feb 15, 1972–Feb 2, 1973
Jan 24, 1936–Feb 10, 1937	Feb 2, 1984–Feb 19, 1985
Feb 10, 1948–Jan 28, 1949	Feb 19, 1996–Feb 6, 1997
Jan 28, 1960–Feb 14, 1961	Feb 6, 2008–Jan 25, 2009

Rats are often charming, sociable, humorous, and strong-willed people, who take any chances offered. They can be greedy and suspicious, and tend to possess great ambition. They are usually gregarious but unpunctual. Because they dislike routine work, they are often found in jobs or professions where each day brings something new. In love, the Rat is most compatible with other Rats, almost equally compatible with Oxen, Dragons, or Monkeys, but not at all compatible with Goats or Roosters. In business, a Dragon is the best partner.

the Ox

Jan 25, 1925–Feb 12, 1926	Feb 3, 1973–Jan 22, 1974
Feb 11, 1937–Jan 30, 1938	Feb 20, 1985–Feb 8, 1986
Jan 29, 1949–Feb 16, 1950	Feb 7, 1997–Jan 27, 1998
Feb 15, 1961–Feb 4, 1962	Jan 26, 2009–Feb 13, 2010

Oxen work hard, go by the book, and are usually methodical and punctual. They tend to be loners and can suffer problems in love and marriage. Continuity is important to them, and they dislike change or interruption. They may be rather slow and stubborn. You will find them performing well in routine jobs everywhere. In love, the Ox will do well with a Rooster or a Pig but should not try a relationship with a Tiger or a Goat. In business, the Ox gets along best with a Horse or a Pig and worst with a Tiger, Dragon, Snake, Goat, Monkey, or Dog.

the Tiger

Feb 13, 1926–Feb 1, 1927	Jan 23, 1974–Feb 10, 1975
Jan 31, 1938–Feb 18, 1939	Feb 9, 1986– Jan 28, 1987
Feb 17, 1950–Feb 5, 1951	Jan 28, 1998–Feb 15, 1999
Feb 5, 1962– Jan 24, 1963	Feb 14, 2010–Feb 2, 2011

Tigers are larger-than-life people: dynamic, full of ideas, and sometimes quarrelsome. They want to be noticed and seem to enjoy complaining, though they can also be extremely generous. They often lead unpredictable lives and make changes for the sake of it. In love, the Tiger is most compatible with the Dragon and slightly less with the Horse; Oxen, Snakes, and other Tigers are worth avoiding. In business, the Tiger will do very well with either Dragons or Horses but should not get mixed up with Oxen, other Tigers, Snakes, Roosters, or Dogs.

the Rabbit

Feb 14, 1915–Feb 2, 1916	Jan 25, 1963–Feb 12, 1964
Feb 2, 1927–Jan 22, 1928	Feb 11, 1975–Jan 30, 1976
Feb 19, 1939–Feb 7, 1940	Jan 29, 1987–Feb 16, 1988
Feb 6, 1951–Feb 26, 1952	Feb 16, 1999–Feb 4, 2000

Rabbits are good listeners with sensitive feelings. They like a quiet life, especially at home, and avoid strong emotions. A Rabbit is likely to be methodical in all things. Light-hearted, Rabbits are good to have around. In love, the Rabbit is perfect with a Dragon and good with a Horse, a Goat, or another Rabbit, and not bad with an Ox, a Snake, a Monkey, a Dog, and a Pig; only the Rooster is incompatible. In business, they are best with another Rabbit, highly compatible with a Rat, Dragon, Snake, Horse, Goat, or Pig, and only in trouble with a Tiger or a Monkey.

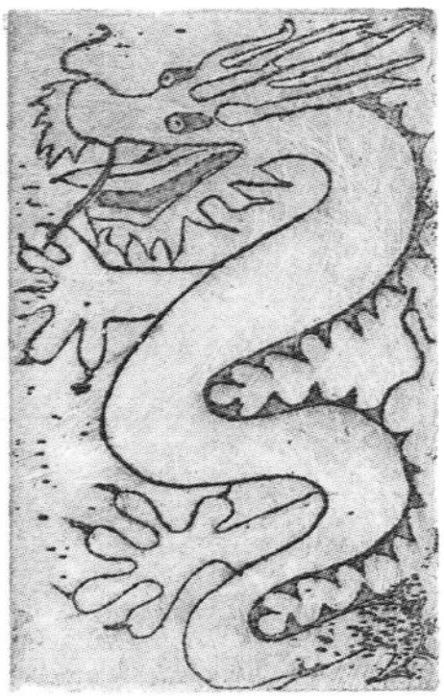

ABOVE Dragons are honest and self-sufficient in all aspects of life.

the Dragon

Feb 3, 1916–Jan 22, 1917	Feb 13, 1964–Feb 1, 1965
Jan 23, 1928–Feb 9, 1929	Jan 31, 1976–Feb 17, 1977
Feb 8, 1940–Jan 26, 1941	Feb 17, 1988–Feb 5, 1989
Feb 27, 1952–Feb 13, 1953	Feb 5, 2000–Jan 23, 2001

Dragons tend to be both admired and hated, good friends and bad enemies. They hate routine. They are often generous but always awkward to deal with, stubborn and demanding. In love, the Dragon is superbly compatible with Tigers, Rabbits, Snakes, Horses, and Monkeys and extremely good with Rats or Goats; only with Dogs or other Dragons are there likely to be serious problems. In business, Dragons do well with Rats, Tigers, Monkeys, Roosters, and Pigs, but should beware of Oxen and Dogs.

the Snake

Jan 23, 1917–Feb 10, 1918	Feb 2, 1965– Jan 20, 1966
Feb 10, 1929–Jan 29, 1930	Feb 18, 1977–Feb 6, 1978
Jan 27, 1941–Feb 14, 1942	Feb 6, 1989–Jan 26, 1990
Feb 14, 1953–Feb 2, 1954	Jan 24, 2001–Feb 11, 2002

The Snake has wisdom and great tenacity. Snakes are very possessive of their loved ones, yet can often be unfaithful. They usually show skill in at least one of the arts, but are prone to making wrong decisions. Snakes are good companions, thanks to their sense of humor, unwillingness to quarrel, and ability to adapt. In love, the Snake is perfect with a Dragon and good with a Horse, and incompatible only with a Tiger or another Snake. In business, they do best on their own, but manage well enough with Rabbits.

the horse

Feb 11, 1918–Jan 31, 1919	Jan 21, 1966–Feb 8, 1967
Jan 30, 1930–Feb 16, 1931	Feb 7, 1978–Jan 27, 1979
Feb 15, 1942–Feb 4, 1943	Jan 27, 1990–Feb 15, 1991
Feb 3, 1954–Jan 23, 1955	Feb 12, 2002–Jan 31, 2003

Horses may be leaders; they are entertaining, humorous and very sensual. Their charm, eloquence, and amiability can be beguiling. They tend to be hard-working but selfish, and make too many changes. In love they are superbly compatible with Goats, Dogs, and other Horses, and good with Tigers, Rabbits, and Snakes. They should avoid Monkeys and Pigs. In business a Horse should choose a Tiger or a Rooster, and almost as good results can be expected with an Ox, Rabbit, Dragon, or Goat; but not with a Rat, a Pig or another Horse.

the goat

Feb 1, 1919–Feb 19, 1920	Feb 9, 1967–Jan 29, 1968
Feb 17, 1931–Feb 5, 1932	Jan 28, 1979–Feb 15, 1980
Feb 5, 1943–Jan 24, 1944	Feb 16, 1991–Feb 3, 1992
Jan 24, 1955–Feb 11, 1956	Feb 1, 2003–Jan 21, 2004

A Goat is likely to be creative and artistic, elegant and peace-loving. Goats are capricious, but their sweet nature and good manners make them popular, not to mention their amorous tendencies. They are easily led, rarely leaders, and undisciplined and poor decision makers. In love the Goat has little control, but will do best with a Horse or perhaps a Rabbit or a Dragon; a Rat, Ox, or Rooster should be avoided. In business a Goat can get along quite well with a Rabbit, a Horse, or a Pig, but not at all with an Ox, a Rooster, or a Dog.

the monkey

Feb 20, 1920–Feb 7, 1921	Jan 30, 1968–Feb 16, 1969
Feb 6, 1932 Jan 25, 1933	Feb 16, 1980–Feb 4, 1981
Jan 25, 1944–Feb 12, 1945	Feb 4, 1992–Jan 22, 1993
Feb 12, 1956–Jan 30, 1957	Jan 22, 2004–Feb 8, 2005

The Monkey is a nimble problem-solver, quick, opportunistic, and often good with figures; but immodest and even vain. Monkeys are intelligent achievers, possessing the potential to be very successful. If they fail, it is due to impatience and inability to share. But they can also be generous and thoughtful. In love the Monkey is highly compatible with Dragons, Pigs, and other Monkeys, compatible with Rats, and completely at odds with Horses or Dogs. The Monkey works well with a Dragon or a Pig, but not with an Ox, Rabbit, Rooster, or Dog.

the rooster

Feb 8, 1921–Jan 27, 1922	Feb 17, 1969–Feb 5, 1970
Jan 26, 1933–Feb 13, 1934	Feb 5, 1981–Jan 24, 1982
Feb 13, 1945–Feb 1, 1946	Jan 23, 1993–Feb 9, 1994
Jan 31, 1957–Feb 17, 1958	Feb 9, 2005–Jan 28, 2006

A frank, sincere, and enthusiastic person, the Rooster tries to be helpful to everyone around them. Roosters can be either miserly or rash spenders. Almost always, they are courageous and self-assured, though sometimes they can be a little pompous or mistrustful. In love only the Ox is compatible with a Rooster, since Roosters are really interested in more permanent relationships. In business the Rooster gets along well with Dragons and Horses and adequately with Oxen, but hardly at all with anyone else.

ABOVE Roosters are artistic, sociable, and extremely strong-willed.

the dog

Jan 28, 1922–Feb 15, 1923	Feb 6, 1970– Jan 26, 1971
Feb 14, 1934–Feb 3, 1935	Jan 25, 1982–Feb 12, 1983
Feb 2, 1946–Jan 21, 1947	Feb 10, 1994–Jan 30, 1995
Feb 18, 1958–Feb 7, 1959	Jan 29, 2006–Feb 17, 2007

Dogs are loyal friends, selfless, faithful, and modest. In their personal lives, they are respectable and discreet; in business they are hard-working. They may be pessimistic or introverted, and often get bogged down with small details. They have very high standards by which they judge themselves and those around them. In love the Dog is wonderfully suited to a Horse or a Pig, but utterly incompatible with a Dragon or a Goat. In business only a Pig will make a good partner; most other partnerships will fail.

the pig

Feb 16, 1923–Feb 4, 1924	Jan 27, 1971–Feb 14, 1972
Feb 4, 1935–Jan 23, 1936	Feb 13, 1983–Feb 1, 1984
Jan 22, 1947–Feb 9, 1948	Jan 31, 1995–Feb 18, 1996
Feb 8, 1959–Jan 27, 1960	Feb 18, 2007–Feb 5, 2008

Pigs are truthful, impartial, and sincere. They are sociable and excellent team members. On the whole, they are cultured and sensitive. They are good decision makers and may be leaders, while their sensual nature can make them good lovers. But they can also be naive and insecure, easy prey for a heartbreaker. In love the Pig is quite compatible with anyone except a Horse, though especially suited to a Dog or a Pig. In business the Pig does best with a Monkey or a Dragon, but should avoid a Horse.

numerology

NUMEROLOGY IS ONE OF THE EASIEST AND MOST STRAIGHTFORWARD SYSTEMS OF DIVINATION, REQUIRING ABSOLUTELY NO SPECIAL APTITUDE OR PSYCHIC SENSITIVITY. EVEN PEOPLE WITH NO TALENT FOR ARITHMETIC CAN MANAGE IT.

All you need to do is to make a simple calculation of your lucky number or numbers – everybody has a name number, sometimes more than one – then look up the prophecies for those numbers.

There are several ways of calculating numbers, usually producing different results, all of which may be significant. For your name number, you should base your calculation on the form of your name that you generally use. In the most commonly used system, the letters are converted to numbers by alphabetical order, and the result is always between 1 and 9.

1	2	3	4	5	6	7	8	9
A	B	C	D	E	F	G	H	I
J	K	L	M	N	O	P	Q	R
S	T	U	V	W	X	Y	Z	

Thus:

J	O	H	N		S	M	I	T	H

1 + 6 + 8 + 5=20 1 + 4 + 9 + 2 + 8=24
2 + 0 = 2 2 + 4 = 6
Total of both names: 2 + 6 = 8

So John Smith's name number is 8.

However, there is an ancient taboo concerning the number 9, which is considered sacred because it is 3 times 3, itself a holy number in many religions. So there is an older, 8-figure system, sometimes called the Hebrew system. If the final total is 9, it is allowed to stand.

1	2	3	4	5	6	7	8
A	B	C	D	E	U	O	F
I	K	G	M	H	V	Z	P
Q	R	L	T	N	W		
J		S			X		
Y							

Using this system:

J	O	H	N		S	M	I	T	H

1 + 7 + 5 + 5=18 3 + 4 + 1 + 4 + 5=17
1 + 8 = 9 1 + 7 = 8
Total of both names: 9 + 8 = 17; 1 + 7 = 8

So John Smith's name number is 8 in the Hebrew system as well.

John Smith's name number is the same using both systems – but this is just a coincidence, as most names will generate different numbers in the two systems. ❧ You can also count just the vowels in the name, which are supposed to show the inner personality; or just the consonants, which are meant to show the outward impression a person gives. John Smith's vowel number is 6, and his consonant number is 2. In the Hebrew system, his vowel number would be 8 and his consonant number 9. ❧ You can calculate your birth number as well. This is based on your day, month, and year of birth. Say you were born on July 14, 1973. You would add 1 + 4 (the day as two separate figures) + 7 (July is the seventh month) + 1 + 9 + 7 + 3, which gives a total of 32. As before, add the 3 and 2, which gives a birth number of 5. Having established your name and birth numbers, you need to see what meanings and prophecies are associated with it. The interpretations are the same for both the 1–9 and 1–8 systems.

meanings of numbers

RIGHT **The sun, moon, stars, planets, and seasons all have symbolic significance in numerology.**

❶ As the first number, this represents the origin, the solitary eminence of the Sun, the creator. It is a powerful and creative number, associated with strong masculinity, and people bearing it may become leaders. It refers very much to the self, so people who have it will be individual, with a tendency to be inventive, determined, and possessed of a pioneering spirit. Along with such power must go responsibility, and unless the person is careful, there is a risk of falling into selfishness, egotism, and severe bossiness. If their schemes fail, they may become aggressive or introverted; even if their schemes succeed, they may become overbearing and ruthless. As a One, your tarot card is The Magician, your lucky days of any month are the 1st, 10th, 19th, and 28th, particularly if one of these coincides with a Sunday or Monday. Your lucky colors are yellow and brown, and your lucky stone is amber or topaz.

❷ Just as One is associated with maleness, so is Two with femininity, being gentle, intuitive, harmonious, and romantic. It is symbolized by the Moon and suggests a mental creativity and an ability to mix well with other people, but an inability to be forceful, to make decisions, or to carry tasks through to their necessary conclusions; more mental power then physical. Your lucky days of any month are the 2nd, 11th, 20th, and 29th, particularly Mondays. Your tarot card is, not surprisingly, The High Priestess. Your lucky colors are the pale, clean ones of white, cream, and green; your lucky stone is moonstone, jade, or pearl.

❸ Threes are creative and disciplined people, associated with the planet Jupiter. Growth, success, luck, happiness, and fertility are suggested, though on the negative side the person may also be gossipy, moody, over-critical, sometimes rather shy or pessimistic or unimaginative, and prone to leaving jobs half done. You will get on especially well with other Threes. Your lucky days are the 3rd, 12th, 21st, and 30th, especially Thursdays. The Empress is your tarot card. Your lucky colors are purple, violet, or mauve, and your stone is amethyst.

❹ There is a completeness in Four, because mathematically it is a square. It is associated with the Earth and its four seasons, and people under its influence tend to be very down-to-earth, systematic, practical, and stable, upholding law and order, using logic and reason in their actions. Yet there is also an earthbound and unimaginative side to these people, who may be over-fussy about small details, lazy, weak, and prone to worrying too much. Occasionally, a Four will have a stubborn, rebellious streak. Friendship is difficult. Your tarot card is The Emperor. Your lucky days are the 4th, 13th, 22nd, and 31st, especially Sundays. Your planet is Uranus. Your lucky colors are blue or gray, and sapphire is your stone.

❺ Under the influence of the planet Mercury, Five represents the senses. There is activity, change, a hatred of routine, a need for novelty, and a reputation for unpredictability. Such people are energetic, adaptable, resourceful, intelligent, and quick to learn. They may be too demanding of others, too impulsive, prone to spreading themselves too thin through too many projects at once. They make friends very easily, but are difficult to live with. If you are a Five, your tarot card is The Hierophant, your lucky days are the 5th, 14th, and 23rd, Wednesdays especially. Any pastel color may be lucky for you. Your stone is diamond.

❻ Six is the number of the emotions, ruled by Venus, planet of love. Mathematically, it is a "perfect number," because it is the sum of its factors, 1, 2, and 3. People under its sway tend to be reliable and well-rounded. There is a love of home, of peace and beauty, and harmony. Sixes tend to be artistic, and good with children and animals. They may also be too sympathetic, too self-sacrificing, too stubborn, too concerned with duty, perhaps too interfering. But they are among the most popular of people, making good friends and partners. Their tarot card is The Lovers, and their lucky days are the 3rd, 6th, 9th, 12th, 15th, 18th, 21st, 24th, 27th, and 30th, especially Fridays – a wide range that suggests they are luckier than most other people. Pink and blue are lucky colors, and the stone is turquoise or emerald.

❼ Seven is the most significant and magical of the numbers. It has long been held sacred, as is shown by the extraordinary frequency of seven in mythology, the Bible, and classifications of all kinds: there are seven notes in the musical scale, seven phases of the Moon, seven seas, seven heavenly bodies in the old Ptolemaic system, seven wonders of the world, seven hills of Rome, seven virtues, seven deadly sins, seven days of creation, seven plagues of Egypt, seven sentences in the Lord's Prayer, seven trumpets in the Apocalypse, and many more. The seventh son of a seventh son is believed to possess great magical powers. People who are Sevens are sometimes great thinkers and may have an occult or psychic side. They may be researchers, investigators, or inventors. Neptune is the ruling planet, so they have an affinity with the sea and often travel widely. But they must use their powers wisely, avoiding pride and cynicism, and accepting that their talents will never make them materially rich. Lucky days are the 7th, 16th, and 25th, particularly Mondays. The tarot card is The Chariot, the color is green, and the stone is moss agate.

❽ Eight comes under the influence of Saturn. Its people will achieve success but not necessarily happiness. They may possess the drive and ability to lead, and thus receive material wealth and recognition, but they can often drive themselves too hard, repressing their feelings, suffering tension, and missing out on satisfying relationships. As an Eight, your lucky days are the 8th, 17th, and 26th, especially Saturdays. Your tarot card is Strength. Any dark color suits you, and your stone is a dark sapphire or an amethyst.

❾ If One symbolizes the beginning, Nine embraces all the previous numbers and symbolizes finality and completeness. Numerologically, it reproduces itself, as the digits of all multiples of 9 add up to 9; for example, $4 \times 9 = 36$, then $3 + 6 = 9$. It is a sacred and mystical number, with many Biblical and legendary references: nine orders of angels, a nine days' wonder, nine points of the law, nine months of pregnancy, nine lives of a cat, and so on. The influence of Mars makes Nines determined fighters; they tend to be compassionate, determined, seekers after perfection; but also self-regarding, impulsive, possessive, and moody. Their friendships tend to be with Threes and Sixes. The tarot card is The Hermit. If you are a Nine, your lucky days are the 3rd, 6th, 9th, 12th, 15th, 18th, 21st, 24th, 27th, and 30th, and your day of the week is Tuesday. Your color is red, and your stones are bloodstone, garnet, or ruby.

John Lennon: how the number 9 affected his life

John Lennon, the musician and songwriter, always believed in the influence of the number 9. He was born on October 9, 1940. His mother's house was 9 Newcastle Road in Liverpool, where John was to write at least three songs which included nine in the title: "One After 909," "Revolution No. 9," and "#9 Dream." The impresario Brian Epstein first saw the Beatles perform live when he attended one of their lunchtime gigs at the Cavern in Liverpool on November 9, 1961. He quickly became their manager, signing their EMI Parlophone record deal on May 9, 1962. The Beatles' first single, "Love Me Do," had the number 4949. John Lennon first met Yoko Ono on November 9, 1966. The Beatles' legal partnership was ended on January 9, 1975. John and Yoko's son Sean was born on John's birthday, October 9, 1975. They lived in an apartment on West 72nd Street, New York ($7 + 2 = 9$). Their apartment number in the Dakota building was also 72. John was shot and killed just outside the building on the evening of December 8, 1980, when it was December 9 back in Liverpool. His body was taken to a hospital on Ninth Avenue.

playing cards

DESPITE ALL THE NEWER AND MORE GLAMOROUS METHODS OF DIVINATION, CARTOMANCY – THAT IS, FORTUNE TELLING THROUGH THE USE OF A DECK OF ORDINARY PLAYING CARDS – IS STILL VERY POPULAR, ESPECIALLY AMONG PROFESSIONALS.

It has been developed and refined over several hundred years, and there are many large and small variations in technique and meaning, with some practitioners using a lot of cards for a reading and others very few.

Divination by cards should not be thought of merely as a mechanical process of turning over cards and reading their meanings. Most professionals employ a good deal of psychic sensitivity or intuition, so that the reading is a kind of clairvoyance, with the cards used as little more than a focus. As with most divination methods, certain customs have developed. These include buying a new deck of playing cards and keeping them solely for cartomancy. Some people prefer not to let anybody touch their cards except for the questioner at the start of a reading, who may be asked to shuffle them and is usually asked to cut the deck, using only the left hand. You may prefer to ignore reversed cards, as some professionals do, especially when using the full 52-card deck. But if you want the added depth of their significance, as in a tarot reading, you should hold the deck with all cards upright and facing you, then mark the top edge by drawing a marker or heavy pencil across it. When conducting a reading, you will probably find it easier in a quiet room so that there are no distractions, preferably with only yourself and the questioner present. There is never a need to rush a reading and always let your own intuition, the overall array of cards, and your knowledge of the questioner guide you. In cartomancy, there is nothing wrong with making three or four spreads and readings for the same questioner at the same session, perhaps using different types of spread, to check that the results are consistent. It is possible to conduct readings using a 32-card deck rather than the complete 52-card one. The 32-card deck is simply one with the twos, threes, fours, fives, and sixes removed. Some of the cartomancy spreads can be done with either the full or the reduced deck. Details of several spreads are given here, but others may be improvised – do not be afraid to experiment. The individual circumstances of the questioner, the feelings of the reader, and the influence of one card on another must all be taken into account.

ABOVE **Playing cards have long been used for both games and divination.**

LEFT **As the foremost card in the suit, the Ace is of prime importance.**

card meanings

These are the meanings of individual cards in the 32-card deck, ignoring combinations.

R = The meaning when the playing card is reversed or inverted

ABOVE The picture cards refer to a person already in your life or about to enter it.

hearts

ACE
Love, satisfaction, happy home life, friendship, romance.
R Unsettled, the end of an affair.

KING
A fair-haired man, kind, affectionate, with good advice.
R A hesitant, unreliable man.

QUEEN
A fair-haired woman, affectionate, faithful, romantic.
R A spiteful and greedy woman.

KNAVE
A happy young person, a good friend, romance.
R Frustration, short temper.

TEN
Great achievement, joy, love – improves cards around it.
R Temporary problems.

NINE
Wishes fulfilled, health and wealth.
R Short-term setbacks, some unhappiness.

EIGHT
Visits, visitors, romance, happy journeys.
R Unrequited love.

SEVEN
Wisdom, imagination, news.
R Boredom, flirtation.

clubs

ACE
Health, wealth, happiness, success, good home life.
R Short-term success.

KING
A dark-haired man, faithful, generous, honest, reliable.
R A troubled man, perhaps dishonest.

QUEEN
A dark-haired woman, very attractive and capable.
R A crafty, unhelpful woman.

KNAVE
A reliable friend, youthful, skilled, helpful.
R Unhelpfulness, insincerity.

TEN
Money coming, a prize or bonus.
R A long trip, perhaps some money coming.

NINE
Immediate results or opportunities, a new lover.
R A disappointing present or result.

EIGHT
A gamble – the proper partner is crucial.
R A poor choice in love bringing unhappiness and financial problems.

SEVEN
Goodwill, friendship, some happiness
R Unhappiness from a small problem.

spades

ACE
Love affairs, passion – be cautious.
R Bad news.

KING
A dark-haired man, doubtful as a friend and dangerous as an enemy.
R A greedy and ambitious enemy.

QUEEN
A dark-haired widow, friendly but unscrupulous.
R A spiteful and jealous woman, also romantic.

KNAVE
A dark-haired young man, rough, well-meaning.
R An untrustworthy friend.

TEN
Unhappiness, worry.
R Similar, involving loss.

NINE
General bad luck, conflict, loss.
R Many misfortunes, though they may be minor.

EIGHT
Threats of trouble, anxiety, obstacles.
R Unhappy news, disappointment in love.

SEVEN
Worries, losses.
R Small problems out of proportion.

diamonds

ACE
Importance, a letter bringing good news, a ring.
R Bad or delayed news.

KING
A fair-haired man, powerful, obstinate, helpful.
R Similar but unhelpful.

QUEEN
A flirtatious and gossipy fair-haired woman.
R Similar but less pleasant.

KNAVE
A fair-haired relative, an official, perhaps selfish.
R A terrible troublemaker.

TEN
Money, journeys, job offers, changes.
R Similar but delayed or problematical.

NINE
A monetary surprise – beware of self-interest.
R Domestic problems, lack of initiative.

EIGHT
A late marriage, a pleasant journey, plans, ideas.
R A hasty, bad late marriage.

SEVEN
News, social chat, surprises.
R Small problems, waste.

the simple answer

If your questioner has a fairly simple and straightforward question that seems to need a quick answer, perhaps just yes or no, here is a very simple spread. Shuffle and get the questioner to cut the deck and then deal the top three cards only. You will need to consider the meanings of each card individually and also how they fit together.

combinations

Combinations of cards have meanings additional to those of the individual cards. For example, if there are many face cards in the spread, this indicates a full and happy social life; a preponderance of hearts suggests love and romance; and a large number of spades is often a bad omen. Four aces signifies a change for the worse; three queens means a meeting of women; two knaves means that people are plotting something.

past, present, future

If you are a beginner to cartomancy, try this simple system. Take a 32-card deck and shuffle well, especially end to end to achieve some reversed cards. Take off the top and bottom cards and lay them face down for later. Cut the remaining 30 cards and deal them face down into three piles of 10: top, middle, and bottom. Turn the piles over one at a time, spreading them into a slightly overlapping row and pushing reversed cards downward, slightly out of line. ❧ The top pile represents the questioner's past, the middle row the present, and the bottom row the future. Then turn over the two remaining cards, which will put a final gloss on your verdict.

the 21-card oracle

This is a more complex and detailed spread. Shuffle and cut the deck, then lay aside the top eleven cards, which are not used. Deal the new top card face down as a "surprise" card for later. Deal the remaining 20 cards carefully so that their upright and reversed positions are retained, laying them face up. Interpret the

.... Upright
.... Inverted

meanings of these, taking special note of any reversed cards. Next, turn over the surprise card and let its meaning play an important role in the interpretation. ❧ For extra detail, gather and shuffle these 21 cards again. Cut and deal into three face-down piles of seven, seven, and six cards respectively. Put the last card aside, face down, as a new surprise. Ask the questioner to choose just one of the piles, then turn and interpret them. ❧ Gather the 20, shuffle, cut, and deal them face down into three piles of seven, six, and six, adding the last card to the existing surprise card. Again, get the questioner to choose a pile, which you turn and interpret. ❧ Finally gather, shuffle, cut, and deal, this time into three piles of six, with the last card going onto the surprise pile. Turn and interpret only the pile of six chosen by the questioner, then finish by turning over the three surprise cards and allowing them to weigh the overall reading.

21st card
(the surprise)

First repeat

Second repeat

Third repeat

Grand surprise

❧ **ABOVE The 21-card oracle is one of the more complex spreads and provides a detailed reading.**

crystallomancy

CRYSTALLOMANCY IS TELLING THE FUTURE FROM THE SHAPES, PATTERNS, AND COLORS SEEN IN A CRYSTAL BALL. IT IS NOW THE MOST POPULAR METHOD OF SCRYING; THAT IS, FORTUNE TELLING BY LOOKING AT A REFLECTIVE SURFACE.

Scrying is one of the oldest methods of divination, practiced since the time of the ancient Egyptians and Babylonians and independently developed in north, south, and central America, and in Australasia.

It must have begun by looking into still water – a pond on a calm day or a bowl of water. Natural pieces of rock crystal have also been used for thousands of years, as well as precious gemstones and other polished stones such as onyx and basalt. Polished metal, glass mirrors, blood, ink, and even soap bubbles have all been mediums for scrying. Today, crystal balls are in common use, though some fortune tellers prefer a hand mirror, preferably small and silver-backed, or a bowl of liquid. ❧ The famous sixteenth-century seer Nostradamus obtained all his prophecies through scrying. His "magic mirror" is usually pictured as a large glass mirror placed upright on a mantelpiece. ❧ The essence of scrying is that you must empty your mind and direct all your attention on the reflective surface, almost hypnotizing yourself with it. If you are lucky, images will appear.

❧ LEFT **Nostradamus is one of the best-known scryers in history, and his prophecies are still avidly debated today.**

choosing a crystal ball

The best kind of crystal ball is one made of **rock crystal** or of **beryl**, though these are rare and usually prohibitively expensive. Most balls are made of **glass**, which is cheaper but can still give good results. It is important that the glass should be clear and free from any flaws or air bubbles. ❧ When choosing a ball, you must inspect it carefully and handle it, to see if it feels right. Never buy one by mail order. In fact, it is supposed to be better if the ball is a gift rather than bought by you for your own use. A ball is generally about 4 inches in diameter, though you can use a larger or smaller one if you prefer. Most are spherical; some have a flattened side to prevent them from rolling; others are oval. ❧ If you do not have a crystal ball, try a **hand mirror**, or a metal bowl nearly full of **water.**

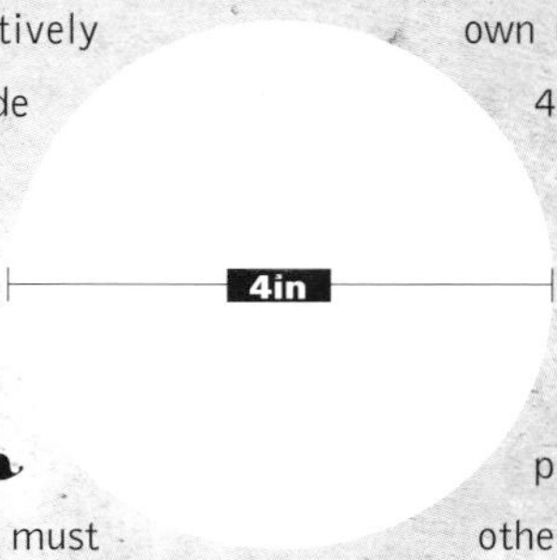

❧ BELOW **If you do not have a crystal ball, use a mirror or a bowl of water.**

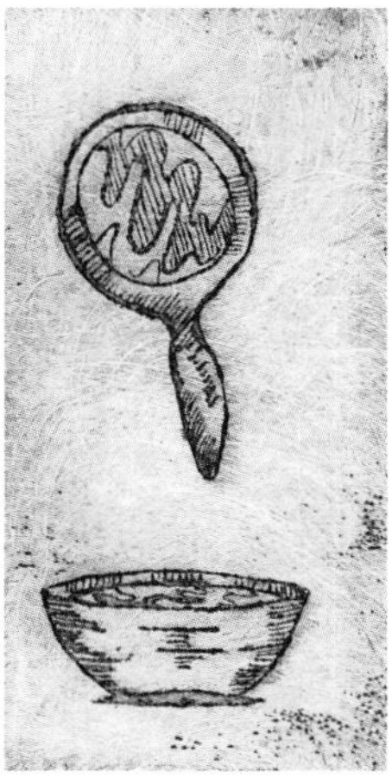

preparation

Careful preparation of your crystal ball is essential. It needs to be washed, preferably in running water from a natural flowing source such as a stream. Some experts recommend either soaking or rinsing the crystal in vinegar. You must polish the ball carefully with chamois leather or velvet, being careful to avoid scratching it, then keep it wrapped in a piece of black silk or velvet. Do not allow sunlight to fall on the ball, or any bright light – though moonlight is supposed to be beneficial. Do not expose it to any extremes of temperature. You may need to tune in or charge up your crystal. This can be done by holding the crystal in your hands and willing it to be charged with your own energy. This procedure is always carried out on a new crystal. You must never allow anyone else to touch your crystal after it has been energized in this way.

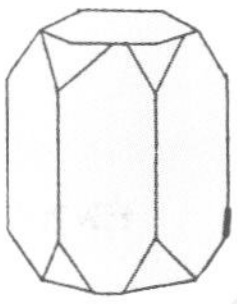

making a reading

Opinions differ as to how, when, and where a reading should be carried out. It is generally agreed that a good time to try scrying is around twilight. Most scryers prefer a quiet, darkened room with no more than two people present, though some will tolerate the noisy surroundings of a psychic fair. Some experts prefer to hold the crystal in their hands, perhaps touching only the black cloth; others support it on a small wooden stand, with a candlestick on each side, all placed on an ornate circular table surrounded by a magic circle chalked or painted on the floor.

❧ Before you begin a reading, it is important that you should enter the correct frame of mind. You must be calm and relaxed. Ask the person for whom you are carrying out the reading to think of their problem or question. They may place their hands close to the crystal for perhaps a couple of minutes; there is no need to touch the crystal itself. Then you look intently into the crystal, making your mind blank so that impressions can enter it. If all goes well, the crystal will appear to turn milky, then as this clears, the true colors and shapes of the reading will appear. Most likely, the images will resemble moving clouds. Color is important here.

color meanings

White	Favorable outlook
Black	Unfavorable outlook
Blue	Happiness
Green	Hope
Yellow	Jealousy
Red Orange	Danger, anger

If the clouds are moving up, a positive answer is indicated; if down, a negative one. A few scryers are able to perceive shapes in the clouds, or even complete scenes. But you may see nothing, for the ability to scry is rare: most people cannot tune in to a crystal and never discern anything useful, however hard they try.

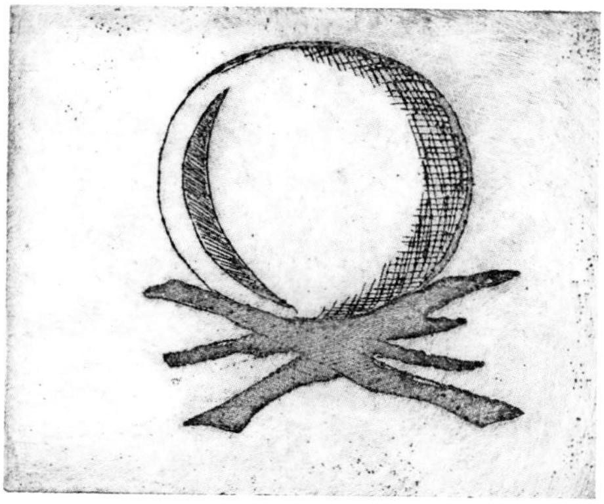

❧ **LEFT A crystal ball is one of the most beautiful and evocative images of fortune telling.**

Dowsing and Pendling

THE POPULAR IMAGE OF DOWSING IS OF A WISE OLD MAN USING A FORKED TWIG TO SEARCH FOR UNDERGROUND WATER. THAT IS TRUE AS FAR AS IT GOES, BUT IT IS FAR FROM THE WHOLE STORY.

Dowsers traditionally hold a thin, Y-shaped hazel twig in both hands while walking across a field, and when water is reached, the twig will point downward without conscious effort by the dowser.

This technique is still used, though some now prefer a twig of another pliable wood. But most modern dowsers use pairs of wire rods. Today's dowser is as likely to be a woman as a man, and the object of the search need not be water. ❧ Dowsing with a pair of wire rods is a simple technique that anyone can try. The rods may be made out of wire coat hangers. They should be L-shaped, with the longer arm about 12 inches long and the shorter one 6 inches. Hold the shorter arm of one rod loosely in each hand; it should point down. The longer arms should be parallel to each other and point forward. Concentrate on what you want to find, and walk slowly forward. When you reach your objective, the ends of the rods will move in and cross; or sometimes they will move away from each other. ❧ The objective may be an underground pipe carrying water or an electrical cable buried in your yard. However, it may also be any mineral substance, from iron ore to buried treasure, or perhaps archaeological remains. You may be astonished by the accuracy of the predictions.

dowsing

Rods will provide specific information, but only as the answer yes or no. Ask your question and keep it in your mind; if the rods move, the answer is yes; if they do not, the answer is no. Some dowsers hold the rods over a recumbent person to find such details as age or IQ. The mechanism is thought to be that the dowser picks up the answer through clairvoyance or telepathy, and that the rods merely amplify a positive response, causing unconscious muscular movements.

pendling

A pendulum can do anything that rods can do – and more. If you suspend it, unmoving, over an object and ask a question, the pendulum will gradually begin to swing in a circle, either clockwise or counterclockwise. These movements stand for yes and no, but not necessarily in that order. Check it with questions to which you know the answers. ❧ An ancient use of a pendulum was for a mother-to-be to suspend her wedding ring above her stomach; if the pendulum swung in a circle, either way, the baby would be a girl, and if it swung back and forth, the baby would be a boy. ❧ The great advantage of a pendulum over rods is that it will give accurate answers when held over a map. It will disclose water, mineral deposits, archaeological sites, and lost items. Answers should always be confirmed by visits to the place itself.

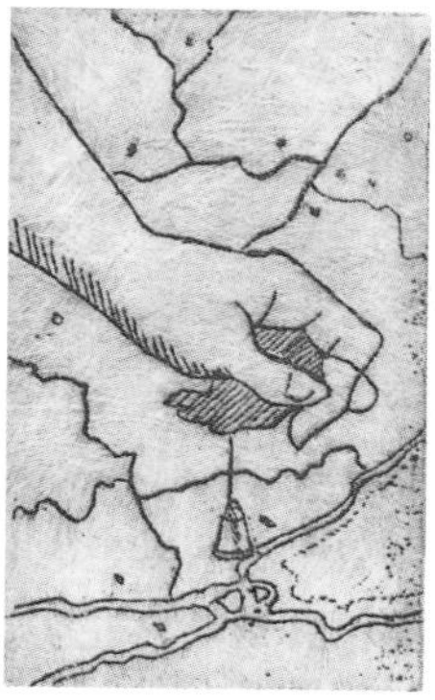

❧ ABOVE **Pendulums have an advantage over rods; they can be held over a map to save the dowser from having to travel to an area.**

DREAMS

EVERYBODY DREAMS EVERY NIGHT, EVEN THOUGH WE RARELY RECALL OUR DREAMS IN THE MORNING. PEOPLE WHO CLAIM THEY NEVER DREAM ARE MISTAKEN: RESEARCH HAS SHOWN THAT WE DREAM FOR ABOUT HALF OUR SLEEPING TIME.

Dreaming is vitally necessary to the normal function of the brain, and it has been said that we sleep in order to dream and that some dreams may contain accurate information about the future.

But first it is necessary to say a few words about non-prophetic dreams. It is clear, from those dreams we do recall, that many – perhaps most – are versions of events that have already happened. We may see people and places familiar to us; or the starting point of the dream may be a television program seen recently, or a novel just read. There is a theory that such dreams clean up and file away the events of the day in memory. Illness may bring particularly vivid dreams, even if the trouble is no more than indigestion. Real events may find their way into dreams: if you feel cold in bed, you may dream of snow and icebergs, or if you hear the doorbell, you may dream that you are answering it.

Dreams as predictions

A small percentage of dreams cannot easily be explained away in these terms. Such dreams may be predictions of future events. Oneiromancy, which means divination through dreams, is a very ancient art. It is described in the **Epic of Gilgamesh**, an ancient Mesopotamian legend which may have originated as far back as 2500 B.C. The Bible has many references to predictive dreams, of which the best known are those interpreted by Joseph in Genesis 40–41. ❧ Belief in the prophetic power of dreams is widespread, found in almost every culture. The ancient Greeks and Romans commonly recorded and interpreted dreams. The Greek writer Artemidoros wrote the first known book on the subject in about A.D. 140. This book gave a rather simplistic symbolism of dream images, which became the standard interpretations that persisted into the nineteenth century. ❧ With the development of experimental psychology in the late nineteenth century, and particularly the publication in 1900 of **The Interpretation of Dreams** by Sigmund Freud, everything changed. Freud asserted that dreams are products of our unconscious mind in a highly symbolic form. He described them as wish-fulfillment fantasies, most frequently with sexual meanings presented in a disguised form. This theory was disputed by the psychologist Carl Gustav Jung, who believed that no single theory could account for all dreams. He dismissed Freud's sexual symbols, but thought it possible that some dreams could be anticipatory or prophetic, and that others could be telepathic messages sent to us by other people, so that the dreamer acquired real information not previously known.

❧ ABOVE **According to the Greek writer Artemidoros, dreaming of a feast meant that good things were in store for you.**

It is unusual for dreams to be clearly predictive. Yet there are a number of extremely common dream elements which most people have probably experienced, and which are thought to have significance. Most dreams are composed of a number of such elements, mixed up with personal recollections. Beware of trying to interpret all elements in a straightforward way, because the subconscious can play tricks, employing puns or metaphors.

NAKEDNESS or some other form of exhibitionism represents shyness and a fear of ridicule, for which our subconscious compensates in the dream. It may indicate that you have something to hide, or will in the future.

FALLING usually indicates that you are worried about something and have doubts about whether you are going to succeed in a particular project. You must not take the falling too literally; it is probably a metaphor for your worry over a relatively small event. Such things are often exaggerated in dreams.

WATER was thought by Freud to represent the amniotic fluid around an unborn child, and thus a desire to return to the womb; but it is now regarded as a metaphor for the emotions. Dreaming of water in any form may refer to hidden problems ahead: serious difficulties if the water is cloudy, emotional changes or even improvements if the water is clear.

A CUP OR CAVE was interpreted by Freud as a vagina; but it is more likely to be a symbol for healing, for coming maturity, or perhaps even for the personality itself. A full cup, or other container, can be interpreted as emotional contentment; an empty cup a general lack of emotional fulfillment; an overflowing cup can indicate that you are being swept along by your emotions and may need to apply some caution.

FOOD in a dream tends to stand for emotional or spiritual nourishment. Food which appears appetizing yet has a disappointing taste may be a warning against satisfying sexual appetites. Overrich food can mean that you are worried about getting more than you bargained for, in any context.

BEING CHASED OR THREATENED, but unable to move, was thought by Freud to represent the paralysis associated with a sexual orgasm; but this is now considered to be a dream of insecurity, a suggestion that something important to you is both desired and dreaded.

A ROAD or path represents the journey through life in general or progress in a current project. If you are moving along confidently and seem sure of your destination, it indicates feelings of security. An uncertain destination indicates an uncertainty in your attitude to life. A wrong or changed destination shows that you are worried by the direction of your life.

FLYING suggests forthcoming success: you are symbolically rising above problems and taking charge over the events which affect you. Alternatively, it may symbolize the process of growing up and the expansion of your horizons. If the flight ends in a fall, this suggests insecurity or the possibility of quarreling with a friend.

OBSTACLES of various kinds in a dream indicate that lack of confidence and inhibitions are preventing you from doing something you want to do and so fulfilling your desires. However, such obstacles may also represent a conflict between what you want do to and what you think it is morally right to do. You need to think carefully before proceeding, as the dream may be revealing a hidden ambivalence toward a specific goal.

CORRIDORS in hotels or trains, with their blank uniformity and impersonality, denote an organization. You are afraid of losing your identity and are, or will be, worried about the effect of some big organization upon you.

WEDDINGS used to be interpreted literally as a prediction of a wedding in the family. Nowadays, it is interpreted in more general terms as a prospective alliance, most likely in the business sense. The other people present in the dream may give some clues to the area of your life represented.

If you want to check on your own dreams, get into the habit of recording them. Keep a notepad and a pencil beside your bed, and be sure to write down all the details of any dream you can remember as soon as you wake up. Date the record and eliminate all obvious recently experienced real events or fictional images. Then scrutinize the remaining dream elements for predictions.

Lincoln's Dream

President Abraham Lincoln had a prophetic dream a few days before he was assassinated in 1865. He dreamed that he was woken up by the sound of people crying and wailing, that he went downstairs in the White House and discovered a corpse in an open coffin in a state room. The face was covered, and he asked who it was. The reply was: "The President. He was killed by an assassin." Then Lincoln woke. He decided to ignore the dream, though if he had taken it seriously he might have avoided the bullets of John Wilkes Booth. After his assassination, Lincoln's body was laid out in that same state room.

Recording Dreams

ABOVE **Recording your dreams in writing as soon as you awake will help you to remember them.**

SUPERSTITIONS

SUPERSTITIONS ARE BELIEFS IN SUPERNATURAL OR AT LEAST INEXPLICABLE EVENTS. OFTEN OF ANCIENT ORIGIN, THEY INCLUDE OLD WIVES' TALES AND FOLK SAYINGS, AND METHODS OF GUARANTEEING GOOD LUCK OR AVERTING EVIL.

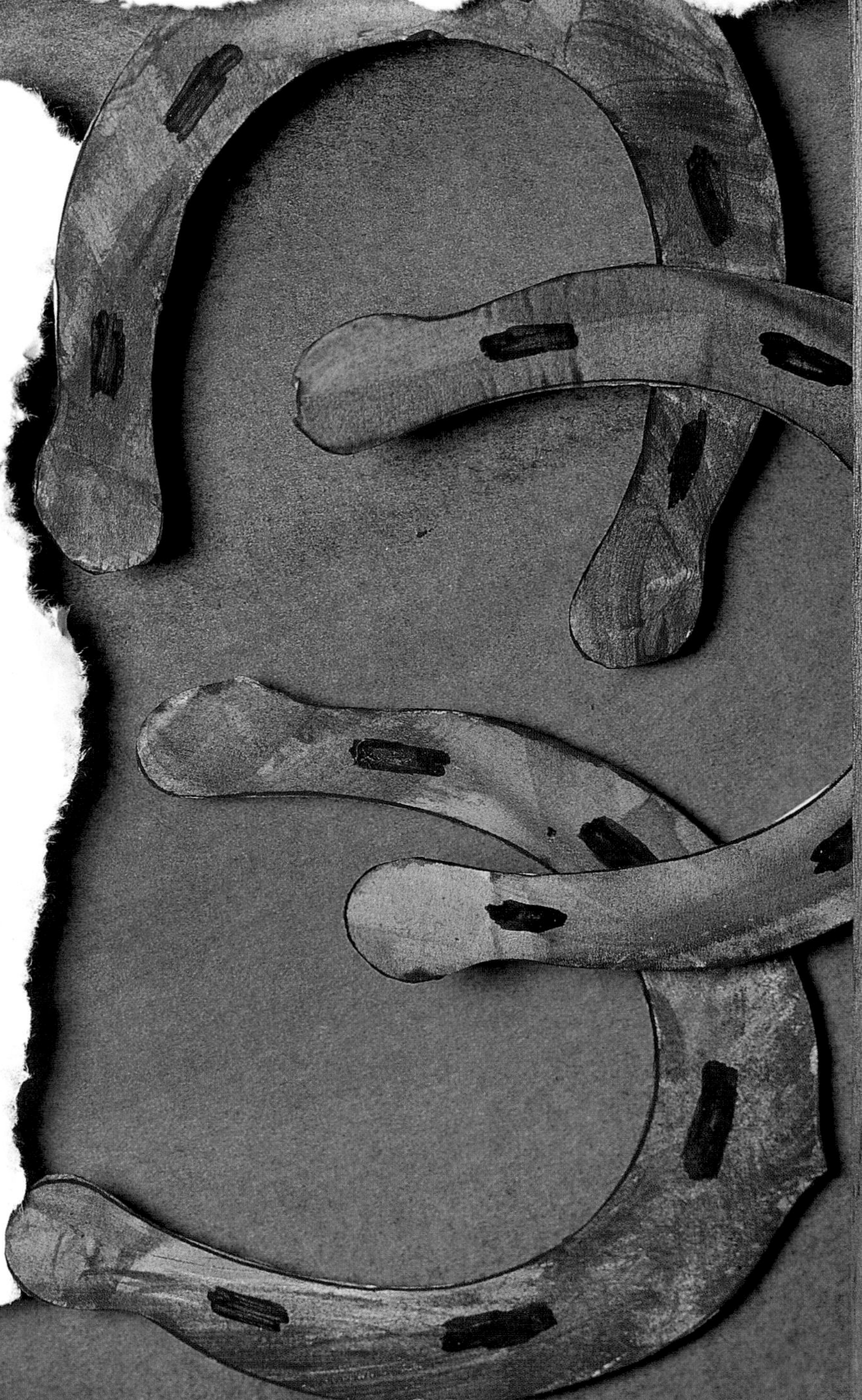

It is in this last sense that superstitions concern divination, for all of us, surely, would love to be blessed with good luck, and many, perhaps even most, superstitions concern omens and signs of future events.

Many superstitions also concern means of bringing about one's desires. For example, a horseshoe can be nailed upright to a door to bring luck. A large number of superstitions are predictions of the weather, varying from the practical to the fantastic, such as the belief that the croaking of frogs and braying of donkeys are signs that rain is on the way. ❧ We can ignore a lot of superstitions that have lost their meaning today, such as the customs and omens connected with haymaking by hand, or the belief that meeting a chimney sweep in the street is very good fortune. Others are beyond the scope of this book, such as herbal remedies. But surprising numbers of useful omens remain and are widely believed, even today, at the end of the rational and scientific twentieth century. Most people will admit to crossing their fingers for good luck at least sometimes.

❧ **LEFT Seeing a chimney sweep was once considered fortunate – nowadays, it would be a rare sight indeed.**

a catalog of superstitions

personal

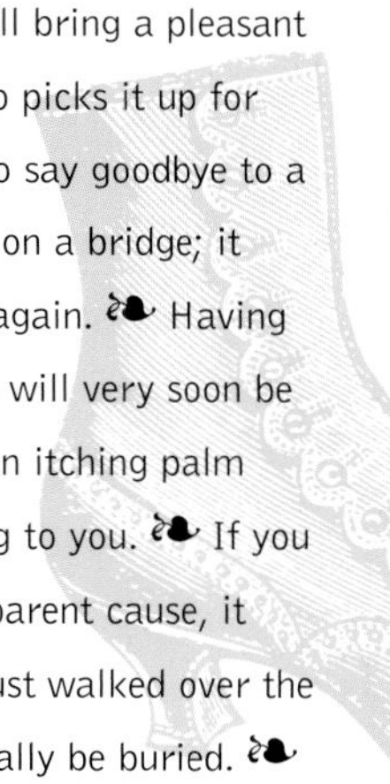

If you drop a glove or a comb, it is bad luck to pick it up yourself, but it will bring a pleasant surprise for anyone else who picks it up for you. ❧ It is very unlucky to say goodbye to a friend while you both stand on a bridge; it means you will never meet again. ❧ Having an itching elbow means you will very soon be sleeping in a strange bed. An itching palm means that money is coming to you. ❧ If you shiver suddenly, with no apparent cause, it means that somebody has just walked over the place where you will eventually be buried. ❧ Never place new shoes on a table, or you will suffer bad luck as long as you wear them.

weather

If you hear the braying of a donkey, it means there will be rain before the day is out. ❧ While rainbows are always a good omen, being able to see both ends of a rainbow at once is especially lucky. ❧ If you see a shooting star in the sky, make a wish quickly while it is still visible and the wish will be granted. ❧ A well-known superstition is that if a groundhog sees his shadow when he comes out on February 2, there will be six more weeks of winter; if he doesn't, spring will arrive early. ❧ Seeing or hearing a woodpecker portends rain. If you notice that ants are unusually busy, it also suggests that rain is on the way.

❧ **LEFT Never put new shoes on a table – keep them firmly on the floor!**

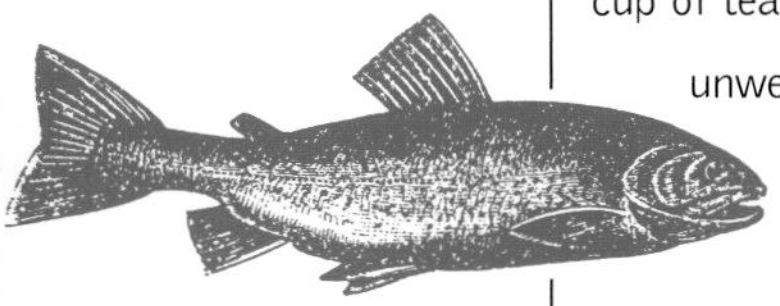

❧ **ABOVE Eat fish from the tail toward the head if you want a good catch next time you go fishing.**

❧ **ABOVE There are many superstitions associated with marriage – to avoid it, a woman should bring snowdrops into the house on Valentine's Day.**

domestic

It is regarded as unlucky to have thirteen people sitting around a table for a meal, but the bad luck may easily be overcome if one of them has a cat on their lap, even if the cat will not stay there long. ❧ If you pour an extra cup of tea by mistake, it means that an unwelcome visitor will arrive soon. ❧ When you are eating fish, always eat from the tail toward the head, then you will have a good catch the next time you go fishing. ❧ If you see milk as soon as you wake up in the morning, it means good fortune; but spilling milk is unlucky. ❧ It is most unlucky to give or receive a pair of scissors without a token payment from the recipient (a single small coin will do). And it is a bad omen to leave a pair of scissors open. ❧ The wishbone from a fowl you have eaten is lucky. Two people should each hold one arm of it and pull until it snaps, making silent wishes as they do so; the one who retains the larger piece will have their wish come true.

love and marriage

If a young woman wants to know the name of the man who truly loves her, she should write the names of all possible contenders on small pieces of paper, cover them thinly in clay and drop them into a bowl of water; the first name to rise to the surface is the one. ❧ Any woman who brings snowdrops into the house on St. Valentine's Day, February 14, will not be married within that year. ❧ If a woman gives a pair of slippers to the man she intends to marry, the marriage will never happen. ❧ Most brides still keep to the old superstitions of dressing for their wedding by deliberately wearing something old, something new, something borrowed, and something blue. They will rarely allow the groom to see the wedding dress before the ceremony or look at themselves in a mirror on the wedding day until after the ceremony. And brides and grooms rarely risk bad luck by seeing each other on the morning of their wedding day.

professions

Many professions have occasional superstitions, but there are two where omens are rife: sailors and actors.

Sailors: A lump of coal found by a sailor on a beach will protect him from drowning. ❧ No sailor will begin a voyage on a Friday, or on the first Monday in April, the second Monday in August, or the last Monday in December. Yet Christopher Columbus sailed for America on a Friday. Sunday is the best day to start a voyage. ❧ Some sailors carry a tiny bag of salt in their pocket for good luck. ❧ Having children on board during a voyage brings luck, but carrying a priest on board is unlucky. ❧ Fishermen hate to be asked when and where they are sailing; they believe that this will adversely affect the size of their catch. ❧ Touching the collar of a sailor will bring anyone luck.

Actors: It is unlucky to say the last line of a play in rehearsal or to whistle in a theater. ❧ To open a new play on a Friday is to ask for trouble. ❧ Shakespeare's **Macbeth** is widely regarded as the most unlucky of plays. It is rarely performed without problems and it is never referred to by name. Actors call it "the Scottish play." ❧ Wearing a wig in a performance is considered lucky.

flowers and plants

The small, daisy-like flowers of bachelor's button, also known as feverfew, should be carried by anybody who wants to know whether their current romance will last. If the flowers stay fresh, so will the romance. ❧ The carnation is a particularly lucky flower and to find a four-leafed clover is regarded as very fortunate. ❧ If you blow on a dandelion head and all the seeds but one drift away, you are in your loved one's thoughts. ❧ Lavender is lucky whether you grow it in the garden or bring it into the house. It is also lucky to grow parsley in your garden, but don't give it away, for your luck will go with it. ❧ It is dangerous to bring snowdrops into the house at any time, for illness or disappointment will enter with them. If you want to give somebody bad luck, give them an orchid as a present. ❧ Dreaming of roses is a very good omen; it brings love and good fortune. ❧ Never pick up any flowers which have been dropped outdoors; it will bring illness to your family.

beasts, birds, and insects

It is regarded as lucky if a bird flying overhead makes a mess on you. (And it is perhaps even luckier for your dry cleaner.) ❧ Hearing a cuckoo calling after the end of July is a bad omen. ❧ To see a fox brings good luck, but to see several together brings misfortune. ❧ Killing a cat brings seven years' bad luck. Killing a robin or a sea gull is also very unlucky. ❧ A rabbit's foot is said to be lucky, and people still sometimes carry one as a good-luck charm. ❧ It is lucky to drive through a flock of sheep on the road. ❧ If rooks build a nest near your house, it is thought to bring luck. Likewise, to have a swallow's nest under your eaves is very lucky. ❧ A bee flying into the house predicts the arrival of good news or of a stranger.

days and dates

Sunday is the most propitious day for beginning any new enterprise. It is the best day to get up after a serious illness. Any article of clothing which is put on for the first time on a Sunday is supposed to last twice as long as it otherwise would. ❧ The Irish consider Monday lucky. But it is unlucky to move house on this day. ❧ On a Tuesday it is very unlucky to meet a left-handed person first thing in the morning. ❧ Wednesday is supposed to be an unlucky day for a child to be born. It is an unlucky day for other beginnings, especially journeys. ❧ Thursday has only one lucky hour, the one before the sun rises. Despite this, if you are determined enough, it is a good day to carry a difficult job through to its completion. ❧ A Friday is most unlucky for beginning a new venture. If you dream on Friday night and tell somebody about it on Saturday, the dream will come true. ❧ Anybody beginning a new job on a Saturday will not stay long. It is a lucky day for baptisms, but not for any dangerous enterprises. ❧ On New Year's Day, it is unlucky to enter somebody's house unless you take along a present for them. ❧ You must take all Christmas decorations down on or before Twelfth Night, January 6, or suffer bad luck. ❧ To preserve your luck, you should make and eat pancakes on Shrove Tuesday, the day before Lent begins.

❧ **ABOVE Roses are a symbol of romance and good fortune.**

❧ **ABOVE A single fox brings good luck, but beware more than one.**

minor methods

THIS BOOK DESCRIBES ALL THE MAJOR SYSTEMS OF DIVINATION AND FORTUNE TELLING CURRENTLY EMPLOYED IN THE UNITED STATES AND EUROPE BUT THERE ARE MANY OTHER METHODS, SOME ANCIENT BUT STILL USED BY A FEW PRACTITIONERS, OTHERS OF QUITE RECENT ORIGIN.

necromancy

The word means fortune telling through communication with the dead. This has been much sensationalized by books and films, but it is normally quite an orderly procedure. It was highly popular a century ago and is still practiced. It is easy to get messages, but they seldom contain much prediction. There are four approaches: spiritualism, clairvoyance, the planchette, and the ouija board. All rely on mental contact between someone in our world and someone who is dead. PLANCHETTES and OUIJA BOARDS are often regarded as party games, but they can produce strange and unexpected results. Indeed, neither should be regarded as a game, and children should not use them unsupervised.

SPIRITUALISM uses mediums to receive messages from the dead. At services in Spiritualist churches, performances in large halls, or séances with only a handful of people, they try to pass on a few comforting words from the dead to those still on this earth. Even if the message is specific, it will most often refer to the past or present.

CLAIRVOYANCE is knowledge of things by supernatural means. Clairvoyants do not specialize in communication with the dead, but in some cases their information appears to arrive in this way. In effect, they use the techniques of the tarot or the crystal ball, but without any help from physical objects. They let their minds go blank and receive flashes of knowledge about their client, sometimes referring to the future. There is probably a touch of clairvoyance in several other forms of fortune telling, including tarot, crystallomancy, runes, and cartomancy. Many people claim sometimes to have known that something was about to happen before it did. If it happens occasionally, we call it intuition; if it happens regularly, clairvoyance.

A PLANCHETTE is a mobile writing device, usually a small board supported on very free-running castors, with a pencil attached. It is placed on a large sheet of paper on a table. Several people lightly rest a finger on the board. Without any of them trying to push or pull it, the planchette will move across the paper, sometimes writing intelligible words, which may be predictions and may come from the dead.

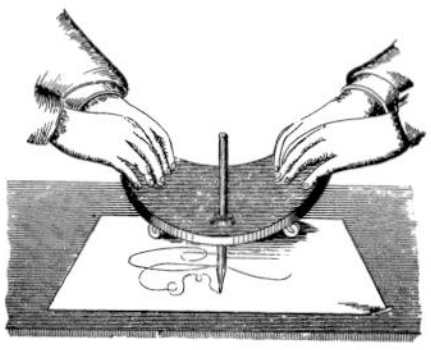

ABOVE 19th-century illustration showing "spirit writing" using a planchette.

THE OUIJA BOARD is a plain, smooth board or tabletop with the letters of the alphabet and a few useful words around the edge. The words always include "yes" and "no," though there may be others – the name is bizarrely derived from the French and German words for yes. On this board is an inverted tumbler, or sometimes a planchette with the pencil removed. The participants rest a finger on this, and it moves from letter to letter, spelling out the words of a message. It is easy to improvise a board with a polished table and letters on pieces of cardboard.

ABOVE Ouija boards are simple to make, but should not be used as a game.

bibliomancy

Bibliomancy has been practiced for thousands of years. It is the simplest of fortune-telling methods; all you need is a book. The Bible is the book most often used – in the past, it was the only book you could be certain of finding in a house. Before this, the writings of the Roman poet Virgil were used; the procedure was known as the **Sortes vergilianae.** First you must concentrate on a particular question or problem. Then open a book at random, open your eyes, and take the answer from the first words that catch your eye, or perhaps the first words on the left- or right-hand page – which of these you choose must be decided before you start. Some people close their eyes and jab a pin into the page, but it is better not to do this if the book is of value.

lithomancy

This method of fortune telling by means of stones requires a candle and a set of eleven semiprecious stones (or pieces of glass) of these colors: blue, colorless, green, red, claret, turquoise, yellow, gray, violet, purple, and black. You must scatter the stones on a flat surface such as a tabletop. Then light the candle and set it in the middle of them. Turn off all other lights in the room, close your eyes, and concentrate. When you open your eyes, the first color you see reflected back at you by the candlelight determines the prophecy, as follows:

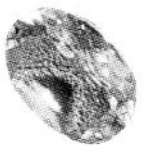

Blue	Good luck
Colorless	Happiness and success
Green	A wish granted
Red	Romance
Claret	Marriage
Turquoise	Opportunity
Yellow	Unfaithfulness
Gray	Sadness
Violet	Grief
Purple	A quarrel
Black	Bad luck

tasseomancy

A similar lack of certainty tends to affect tasseomancy, prediction by means of the patterns of tea leaves left at the bottom of a cup. The name is a derivation from the French **tasse**, cup, and the Greek **manteia**, prophecy. It is best to use a teacup – not a mug – of plain white china, since any colored pattern or fancy shape makes reading more difficult. The tea should be of a large-leafed type, such as Earl Grey. ❧ Drink some tea from the cup first, so that the prediction will apply to you. Leave some liquid at the bottom to cover the leaves. Hold the cup in your left hand and, while thinking of a question or problem, swirl the contents three times counterclockwise. Turn the cup upside down over a saucer so that all the liquid runs off and allow it to drain for a few seconds, then right the cup and inspect the leaves. ❧ There is significance in the pattern, if any, and the position of the leaves. Examine the cup from different angles, half-closing your eyes to make any pattern more prominent. Hundreds of different shapes and their symbolic meanings are listed in some books. These are some of the most common:

Arch	A happy marriage or a change for the better
Bottle or eye	A warning
Bird	Good luck or good news coming to you
Crescent moon	A love affair is coming
Ship	A journey, good tidings from overseas
Tree	Ambitions fulfilled
Triangle	Work hard and you will succeed
Egg	Fertility

The handle of the cup represents you, the inquirer, so any shapes close to the handle will affect you; while shapes on the other side of the cup will affect other people and places away from your home. The bottom of the cup is an unlucky area, and shapes here bode misfortune. ❧ It is possible to use a similar procedure with coffee grounds, though their fineness makes reading even more uncertain. Some European countries have an old tradition of studying the shapes formed by molten wax or lead dropped into cold water, particularly on New Year's Eve, to obtain predictions for the year ahead.

pyromancy

Fortunes may be told by several different methods involving fire and burning. This is a very ancient method, probably prehistoric. Looking for shapes in the embers of a fire used to be a favorite diversion for children, but central heating has reduced its popularity. This is best done quietly in a darkened room, with a fire that has burned down to a mass of glowing coals. Throw a small handful of salt on the embers and, when the flames have died down again, look hard for any recognizable shapes. The usual interpretations are:

Cat, clover leaf, mountain, or pair of shoes	Good luck
Eagle, flower, hatchet, or sword	Bad luck
Pillar or any kind of tree	A coming love affair

A century ago, it was popular – again, particularly among children – to write a wish on a small piece of paper and throw it into a fire in the grate. If the paper burned up, you did not get your wish, but if it was caught by the hot air and carried up the chimney, you would be lucky. This technique is still occasionally practiced. ❧ Another variation is for several people each to mark a stone and place it in a fire. The next morning, the stones are retrieved and examined. An undamaged stone brings luck. This used to be a Halloween custom in some places.

lychnomancy

The name means divination by lamps. You can do it using a single candle. Stare at the flame and ask a question, preferably unspoken to avoid breathing on the flame. If the flame rises, the answer is yes; and if it falls, the answer is no. Another method is to use three candles. Concentrate on the behavior of the flames, which may be interpreted thus:

One of the candles goes out suddenly without obvious cause	Beware of a disaster
One or more flames rises and falls	Danger is approaching
One flame twists and spirals	Your enemies are plotting against you
Sparks rise from a flame	Be cautious
A flame moves from side to side	You are soon likely to travel
One or more wick shows a glowing point	Your luck is in
One flame is brighter than the other two	Good fortune will come to you

❧ **BELOW Children used to study the shapes formed by the dying embers of a fire.**

❧ **LEFT The inner bowl of the cup should be plain white so that the pattern of the tea leaves is easy to see**

SORTILEGE

This means divination by the casting of lots. It used to be carried out with marked pebbles, then later with dice or occasionally dominoes. Today it is uncommon and seems to be practiced only with dice. The most common method is to draw a 12-inch circle, then take three standard dice, each six-sided and marked 1 to 6, shake them, and cast them into the circle. If one comes to rest outside the circle, your plans may be upset; if two do, expect quarrels. From the dice which do land in the circle, count the total of spots on the uppermost face of each. Whatever the total, there is a divinatory meaning:

BELOW The easiest way to practice sortilege is by using three standard dice.

- **3** A surprise, luck
- **4** Unpleasantness
- **5** A wish will come true
- **6** A loss
- **7** Scandal or problems in business
- **8** You will be affected by external influences for good or evil
- **9** Love and marriage
- **10** Birth
- **11** Illness or a parting, possibly even death
- **12** Good news
- **13** Expect grief
- **14** You will get help from a friend
- **15** Be very cautious
- **16** You will soon travel
- **17** Your plans will be changed
- **18** Expect great success

A simple variation is to divide the circle into 12 equal slices. Going around clockwise from 12, these areas refer to: enemies, friends, work, state of mind, legal affairs, love and marriage, health, the present, domestic affairs, travel, money, and next year. Throw one or more dice into the circle. Each number thrown has the following interpretations, which should be applied to the area in which each die lands.

FAR RIGHT Mark out a circle and throw the dice over it to determine how a particular area of your life will progress.

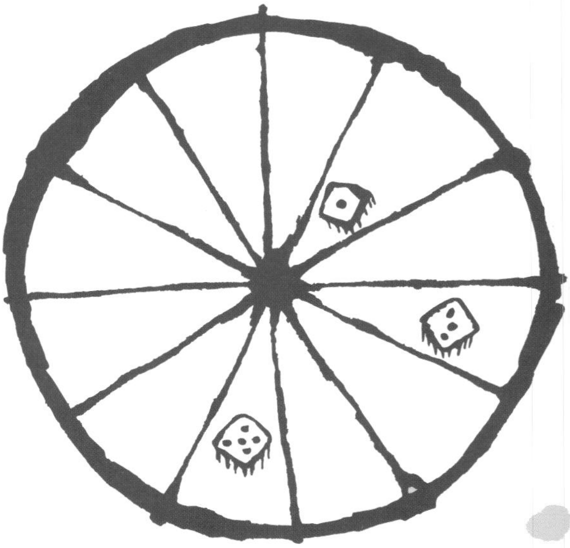

- **1** Good on the whole
- **2** Any success you achieve depends on other people
- **3** Great success
- **4** Some problems
- **5** Indications of a favorable result
- **6** Uncertain prospects

index

Credits

Key: a above; b below; c center; l left; r right

ET Archive 9bl & br; Images Colour Library 15cr; Fortean Picture Library 19cr; Ann Ronan Picture Library 23b & cr; ET Archive 29cr, 30cl; Ann Ronan Picture Library 30a, 31a, 38al; ET Archive 45ar; Mansell Collection 49a & r; Ann Ronan Picture Library 49c; Mark Stevens 52bl; Mansell Collection 53cr; Ann Ronan Picture Library 55c, 57ar, 59ar; Mauritius/Ace Photo Agency 59br; Ann Ronan Picture Library 60cl, 61ar.